SORRY WORKS

Disclosure, Apology, and Relationships
Prevent Medical Malpractice Claims

Doug Wojcieszak

James W. Saxton, Esq.

Maggie M. Finkelstein, Esq.

authorHOUSE®

AuthorHouse™
1663 Liberty Drive, Suite 200
Bloomington, IN 47403
www.authorhouse.com
Phone: 1-800-839-8640

First published by AuthorHouse 3/10/2008

ISBN: 978-1-4343-7713-5 (sc)

Printed in the United States of America
Bloomington, Indiana

This book is printed on acid-free paper.

James W. Saxton is co-chair of the Health Care Department and Chair of the Health Care Litigation Group. He is an active trial lawyer — a practice he has sustained for over 25 years — representing providers, including physicians, hospitals, and retirement communities in state and federal courts and administrative proceedings. His practice includes litigation, risk engineering, and many aspects of health law.

Mr. Saxton uses his extensive experience as a litigator to advise hospitals, medical groups, and retirement communities throughout the United States in connection with understanding and reducing their professional liability risk. He develops risk reduction strategies for health care providers and organizations nationwide and has created innovative solutions and educational programs to support them based on data and collaboration with thought leaders in the healthcare industry. This includes the creation of completely customized specialty-specific assessment tools and management systems for self-insured organizations, captive insurance programs, and reinsurers. Mr. Saxton also provides exceptional education and training on disclosure and apology that help providers benefit from such a strategy with legal entanglements.

Mr. Saxton has published more than 200 articles, several handbooks, and seven textbooks. His recent work includes *The Satisfied Patient, Second Edition: A Guide to Preventing Malpractice Claims by Providing Excellent Customer Service; Five-Star Customer Service: A Step-by-Step Guide for Physician Practices; and 15 Policies and Procedures to Reduce Liability for Physician Practices*. In addition, Mr. Saxton has created multiple educational films and participates regularly in national teleconferences on these issues. He also sits on several editorial boards.

Mr. Saxton lectures frequently and is an invited speaker across the country on health care issues, including liability reduction, risk management, and disclosure. He is invited to nationally prominent healthcare organizations such as the American College of Surgeons, the American Society for Bariatric Surgery, the American Health Lawyers Association, the American Society for Healthcare Risk Management, the Medical Group Management Association, the American Association of Clinical Urologists, and the National Professional Education Institute.

Mr. Saxton is the immediate past chair of the American Health Lawyers Association's Healthcare Liability and Litigation Practice Group and a member of numerous professional associations. As published in the June 2005 issue of *Philadelphia* magazine, he was recognized as a 2005 Pennsylvania Super Lawyer by being selected by his peers as among the top 5 percent of lawyers in the Commonwealth.

Maggie M. Finkelstein concentrates her practice in health law with a focus on loss control, event management, and disclosure for physicians, hospitals, staff, and long-term care communities. She has developed risk reduction opportunities in the health care industry. Ms. Finkelstein has conducted research and analysis of various risk management and liability risk issues, including the risks associated with bariatric surgery, gastroenterology, and obstetrics. She also is a member of the Litigation Group, litigating in both federal and state courts, defending physicians, hospitals, and long-term care communities.

Ms. Finkelstein is a member of the American Health Lawyers Association and regularly publishes on loss control, risk management, and disclosure topics, including books, handbooks, and book chapters. Her recent work includes *Five-Star Customer Service: A Step-by-Step Guide for Physician Practices* and *15 Policies and Procedures to Reduce Liability for Physician Practices*, both published by HCPro, Inc. Ms. Finkelstein is also the co-author of the chapter "Enabling Patient Involvement Without Increasing Risks" in the book *Partnering with Patients to Reduce Medical Errors* published by AHA Press and the chapter "Opportunities for Loss Control in an Alternative Risk Financing Structure" in the book *Alternative Risk Financing Options for Healthcare Organizations* published by the American Health Lawyers.

Prior to joining Stevens & Lee, she was a law clerk for the Honorable William W. Caldwell in the U.S. District Court for the Middle District of Pennsylvania and worked as a chemistry technician and microbiologist at Johnston Laboratories. Ms. Finkelstein is also a registered patent attorney with the U.S. Patent and Trademark Office.

Doug Wojcieszak is a public relations consultant who has had several personal and professional experiences with tort reform and medical malpractice issues. He lost his oldest brother to medical errors in 1998, and his family successfully sued the hospital and doctors, with the case settling in 2000. The hospital attorneys apologized to Wojcieszak's family, but only after the case was settled and money exchanged hands, and they never admitted fault for the incident.

Around the same time his brother's case was concluding, Wojcieszak left his employment with the Illinois House Republicans and accepted the position of executive director of Illinois Lawsuit Abuse Watch (I-LAW), a grassroots, pro-tort reform group. He was able to place over 200 positive stories about lawsuit abuse and capping lawsuit damages with TV, radio, and print media throughout Illinois. During his time with I-LAW, Wojcieszak also first read and studied full-disclosure methods for medical errors as a way to lower malpractice lawsuits and liability costs as well as reduce medical errors.

Wojcieszak left I-LAW in 2001 and returned to the Illinois House Republicans for a brief stint, after which he founded a public relations consulting firm: Tactical Consulting. The firm has had several clients, including a pro-plaintiffs group, Victims and Families United (VAFU). Wojcieszak served as the group's spokesperson in 2004 and touted traditional plaintiffs/anti-tort reform messages such as insurance reform and increased doctor discipline. However, while representing VAFU, Wojcieszak revisited full-disclosure methods and created a marketing term — "Sorry Works!" — to successfully promote apologies for medical errors as the solution to the medical malpractice crisis.

Wojcieszak was able to place over 50 stories about Sorry Works! during 2004 with numerous media outlets, including the *Chicago Tribune*, *St. Louis Post-Dispatch*, and CNBC, and a worldwide story through the Associated Press. He noticed that Sorry Works! while agreeable to many trial lawyers, also attracted the interest and support of many doctors and insurers. These observations led Wojcieszak to create a new, separate group — The Sorry Works! Coalition — in February 2005 solely dedicated to promoting Sorry

Works! and full-disclosure methods as a middle-ground solution to the malpractice crisis. He currently serves as the group's spokesperson.

The Sorry Works! Coalition has grown quickly to over 2,500 members nationwide, the website has received over four million hits, and the group has been publicized in countless popular and trade publications, including *Time Magazine*, *National Review*, *National Law Journal*, and *American Medical Association News*.

Sorry Works! has become the nation's leading organization advocating full-disclosure as a middle-ground solution to the medical malpractice crisis, and the group's website has become the site for information and updates on the full-disclosure movement.

In his speeches on Sorry Works! Wojcieszak teaches healthcare, insurance, and legal professionals what patients and families want most after adverse events and bad outcomes: honesty, accountability, communication, and a real commitment to fix problems. Wojcieszak has given his talks to prominent medical, healthcare, and insurance organizations throughout the United States.

CONTENTS

Acknowledgement

The authors wish to personally thank each reader for their interest in this important topic. It is our hope that the information and strategies in this book will allow physicians, nurses, all clinicians, hospitals, long-term care facilities, healthcare organizations, insurers, and attorneys to embrace enhanced communication and disclosure after an adverse event. The benefit will inure not only to all of these healthcare individuals and facilities, but also to your patients, residents, and their families.

Special thanks are extended to Stevens & Lee, who has truly made a commitment to not only represent healthcare professionals, but also to understanding how important topics like safety and communication can impact their practice and business. Thanks to members and friends of The Sorry Works! Coalition for their strong support of this endeavor and their consistent efforts to further the disclosure and apology movement. To the many individuals who provided assistance, particularly Gynith Shaeffer and Amy Matthias of Stevens & Lee, we extend our thanks.

Many thanks are also extended to Press Ganey, particularly Matt Mulherin and Dr. Melvin Hall; Neil Hutcher, M.D.; Pat Sedlak (Director, AON Risk Services); Ilene Corina (President, Pulse of NY); and Flip Corboy, Esq. for their contribution and review of the book. Each of them are not only highly respected colleagues, but also friends.

We thank our very talented artist, Sally Saxton, who created the book illustrations, capturing many of the critical moments in time. As they say, a picture paints a thousand words. Use them as reminders of this important topic.

Ms. Finkelstein personally thanks her husband (fiancé at the time this book was conceptualized) for his strong support and interest as well as her parents and siblings for their support throughout the years.

Mr. Wojcieszak personally thanks Dr. Steve Kraman for his guidance, honest opinions, and friendship over the last four years. Mr. Wojcieszak also thanks his wife, brother, and business partner for all of their support, and a special thank you to Mom and Dad for always teaching that good can come out of bad.

FOREWORD

BY JAMES W. SAXTON, ESQ.

CHAIRMAN, HEALTH CARE LITIGATION GROUP

CO-CHAIR, HEALTH CARE GROUP

STEVENS & LEE

E-MAIL: JWS@STEVENSLEE.COM

Sorry Works! . . . works, but don't think about it as a name, but rather as a concept. It really does work. Concern about the concept most likely stems from confusing the concept of showing empathy and compassion versus an apology where one accepts responsibility. Both are important concepts, but are very different. Many lawyers, risk managers, and insurance professionals thought that "sorry" meant one was somehow admitting liability or that they had done something "wrong," perhaps accepting responsibility. This concern was enough to make many pause . . . some from even interacting with patients and family after an unfortunate outcome. Laws even had to be passed so doctors could say, "I'm sorry," without being somehow made to also have admitted fault.

We've been making it too hard. Sorry Works! works when there is an adverse outcome. Everyone is sorry, as they should be. Everyone wants to show empathy, which is a basic human response and need. It is a little sad that this concept has become at all controversial. Admittedly, with the phrase, "I'm sorry," there is room for misinterpretation, all the way around and probably in good faith. A doctor could misinterpret the concept, thinking this means he or she is accepting responsibility for a known complication of a procedure or for failing to meet patient expectations. That is not the case. Patients may think "I'm sorry" means that someone did something wrong. Insurance companies may think it means that they will be required to make a payment. These conclusions underscore the importance of education and institution of a process and a program.

To be clear, "sorry," or showing empathy, *works* by making a difficult situation a little better nearly 100% of the time. It does not mean the pain, discomfort, and expenses that go along with an adverse outcome will go away. Of course not. It does not mean 100% of the time the patient will not go to a lawyer or not pursue a lawsuit. However, it does make these very difficult situations a little better almost 100% of the time. "Sorry" works.

At times, an apology and literally accepting responsibility for an error needs to happen. An apology that includes acceptance and ownership is powerful and important and far better than the alternative of years of contentious public litigation in many situations. However, it is admittedly more complex. Sometimes it is hard to quickly determine fault (meaning responsibility). In America and other similar countries where there is not a "no-fault system," we need to be thoughtful about the method. Further, once we accept responsibility, sometimes it is difficult to determine value. Determining value for inherently subjective damages is challenging, but can be accomplished. Do lawyers help? Maybe, but not all the time. Some would argue that the transactional cost of a settlement with a lawyer has climbed rather high. If we had the 50% transactional costs and expenses and settled with a family three years earlier, we could certainly do a lot of good. However, sometimes lawyers do help, a lot.

Think of Sorry Works! first as a concept...the act of kindness, caring, and reaching out to the patient and family after an adverse event. Part of that process will be expressing sorrow: "I'm sorry." We will show you how this can be done appropriately without admitting fault prematurely. We will show you how it actually makes the entire situation better for the providers if the event moves forward to litigation. We will also explain when it is appropriate to apologize and accept responsibility, and how to do it.

Let's not get bogged down with why it may not work, but instead talk about how we can thoughtfully make it happen. Doug Wojcieszak knows firsthand, and the hard way, how badly Sorry Works! is needed. He and his family went through it. In the first chapter of this book, he will share with you the importance of this concept. Our team of healthcare litigators, along with risk managers, surgical consultants, psychologists, and physicians, in collaboration with insurers and hospitals across the country, has dealt with this issue time and time again. The Sorry Works! Coalition and Stevens & Lee have collaborated to put forth a straightforward book on this concept often referred to as disclosure, and a concept we feel is really a subset of enhanced communication post-adverse event. We will go through what Sorry Works! is and what it is not - why it works and most importantly how. We have done so only after seeing it work for many, many doctors, hospitals, insurers, and, of critical importance, patients. We have talked to the "naysayers" and worked through the concept with them as well. Many have found out how important this concept is the hard way — in court. You need not.

There is work to be done with Sorry Works! by doctors, insurers, hospitals, and yes, patients. There is clearly a job for patients here. We must get patients on the same side of the table as our doctors post-adverse event. It really works better when, at least initially, patients go to their doctors first. Also, it is important to understand that Sorry Works! or disclosure and apology does not just happen. Like so many things in life, there needs to be a process, a method, a plan, and execution steps. That is where this book can help.

If you ever sat through a meeting with a doctor and a patient after heartfelt empathy is exchanged with everyone in the room crying and yet everyone in the room feeling better, you would understand that "sorry" works for everyone. Let's get started.

PREFACE
BY DOUG WOJCIESZAK

This book is, in part, adapted from speeches I have given to medical, insurance, and legal organizations across the United States and in Australia and Canada over the last two years. Liability exposure has been a major issue for healthcare and insurance professionals for a long time, and they are looking for new solutions to an old problem. More and more doctors, nurses, risk managers, hospital administrators, and insurance executives are turning to Sorry Works! for answers. I thought it was time to put Sorry Works! in a book that was concise and to the point. Along the way I met and had the pleasure of working with James Saxton and his team at the law firm of Stevens & Lee. It was fascinating to me how as lawyers and health law consultants they were spreading the same message. To make sure this message was well grounded in law and risk management principles, we collaborated, and this book is part of that partnership. This book adequately covers the topic of disclosure and apology but has intentionally been kept short so even the busiest professional could read it on a plane ride or over a weekend.

Though Sorry Works! has its roots in medicine, it is my hope that this book finds a wider audience in corporations, the small business community, and other sectors of our society that are concerned about litigation. I also hope the book appears in college course syllabi so future doctors, lawyers, and business people can read, discuss, and debate it. Indeed, if Sorry Works! can *work* in medical malpractice (often thought to be one of the most contentious and expensive litigation arenas) imagine what it can do elsewhere! Moreover, though Sorry Works! is a process and program, it also a way of life universal to all people. Indeed, Sorry Works! returns us to our parents' lessons about apology and fixing mistakes.

People can actually live with mistakes, but they do not accept or tolerate cover-ups. Sorry Works! taps into this psyche and, in doing so, provides a simple yet devastatingly effective way to reduce litigation and associated expenses while improving outcomes and safety, which further decreases litigation exposure. The keys are honesty, candor, and a real commitment to fix problems when something goes wrong. All three elements must be present to prevent conflict, and Sorry Works! shows you how to do it.

I hope you find this book useful as well as enjoyable and welcome your feedback at doug@sorryworks.net or by calling 618-559-8168. Thank you!

Doug Wojcieszak
Founder/Spokesperson
The Sorry Works! Coalition
www.sorryworks.net

CHAPTER 1
SORRY WORKS! WHEN IT ALL STARTED

On May 5, 1998, my oldest brother, Jim Wojcieszak, walked into a Cincinnati, Ohio hospital at two in the morning complaining of chest, shoulder, neck, and stomach pains. Jim was a big, burly man…the kind of guy who was asked to play football in high school, so he shouldered pain extremely well. For Jim to show up in an emergency room at 2:00 a.m. with no prodding from Mom and Dad meant he was in *excruciating* pain.

Jim told the attending physician he was either having the worst case of indigestion he had ever had or he was suffering a heart attack. Jim had a temperature of 101.4° F, and the physician detected a "slight" heart murmur. Jim told the physician he had no history of heart murmurs. The physician told my brother that at age 39 he was too young to be having a heart attack, and he must be suffering from indigestion or stomach flu. However, the physician never drew blood to rule out a heart attack — he just assumed because of my brother's age and physical appearance that nothing was amiss. How we wish he had been right.

The doctor started an IV for the pain and also administered an ulcer cocktail. Jim's pain persisted, but they released him anyway at 5:45 a.m. A few hours later, Jim called my parents complaining that he could not sleep. He could not lay on his back or his side; the pain was simply too great. Furthermore, he was coughing and spitting up blood. Mom and Dad quickly picked up Jim and took him to their family physician.

Our family physician became excited quickly. He said the emergency room "dropped the ball." Jim didn't have a "slight" heart murmur — he had a significant heart murmur. Moreover, the oxygen levels in Jim's blood were dangerously low. Our doctor said that Jim would probably be in the ICU by that evening, and he sent Jim and my parents back to the same hospital.

Back to the hospital they went. My father dropped Jim and Mom off at the emergency room and parked the car in a lot far from the hospital. Jim and Mom walked into the emergency room, but there was no one there to greet them or help them. Mom told Jim to sit down in the waiting room, and she walked quickly down a long hall to the main entrance of the hospital to get help, but no one was at the hospital's main reception desk either. So, she went back down the long hall to the emergency room waiting area, where she bumped into two nurses who were bringing in coffee. Around this time, Dad finally arrived from the parking lot, and both he and Mom noticed that Jim had fallen asleep in the waiting room because his oxygen levels were so low. My parents were shocked and upset at how there was a total lack of urgency in the emergency room.

Jim was eventually admitted, and this time the hospital staff drew Jim's blood, and, sure enough, the enzyme was present in the blood showing the heart was in distress. When quizzed by my dad why blood was not drawn when Jim was in the emergency room at 2 a.m., an ER resident quipped, *"Remember, this is the art of medicine, and Jim is a young man."*

The doctors told my parents that Jim had a bacterial infection of the heart that was attacking his mitral valve. They had begun administering a broad spectrum of antibiotics, and surgery may be needed in several weeks to repair damage, but only after the bacterial infection had cleared. Jim was admitted to the ICU.

The ICU was the site of a second, serious mistake. The computer monitor over Jim's bed read *"Ray Wojcieszak."* Who's Ray? That's my dad. This was a critical fact because Dad had a heart stress test performed in the same hospital a few months prior to Jim being admitted, and even though Dad was in his sixties at the time, the cardiologist said he had the heart of a 30-year-old man. No blockage. Low cholesterol. Excellent cardiac health.

So, there was my dad arguing with the attending physician about who was who — the attending physician was convinced that Ray was in the bed — and having to produce driver's licenses to prove he was indeed Ray and the man in the bed was Jim. The staff changed the name on the computer monitor to read *"Jim Wojcieszak,"* but we believe they were still probably looking at Dad's charts showing no blockage, low cholesterol, and excellent cardiac health. In short, they used Dad's charts to form their diagnosis of a bacterial infection of Jim's heart.

Later that evening, the physicians prescribed nitroglycerin for the pain in Jim's chest and back, but the pain persisted. In fact, Jim could not lie down in a bed. Laying on his side or back was excruciatingly painful. So, they propped him up in a special chair, but the pain still continued. They said the antibiotics needed time to clear the bacterial infection and the pain would decrease over time.

The next morning, the attending physician and a cardiac specialist visited and informed Jim and my parents that a valve would need to be replaced in his heart once the bacterial infection cleared. However, they assured our family that a valve replacement was a *"straightforward"* operation and not to worry. Shortly after the physicians left, the nurse told Jim he would soon receive lunch, which made him happy because he was very hungry. Two hours later lunch had still not arrived. When my parents called the nurse to inquire about lunch, she told them it had been forgotten.

After eating lunch, Jim needed to use the bathroom for a bowel movement. He beeped the nurse, and she came down to his room — but she was not the regular nurse. The substitute nurse helped Jim out of bed and had him walk across the room to the bathroom, and then she helped him walk back to his chair after using the bathroom. Shortly after she left, Jim started coughing and spitting up blood. When the oxygen sensor was put back on his finger, alarms went off and his regular nurse increased his oxygen levels, but Jim still had trouble breathing.

Later that afternoon, Jim tried to use the bathroom again, this time to urinate, and his regular nurses caught him and gave him a tongue lashing for walking in his room. She informed him that ICU patients in his condition do not get out of bed. So, why did the substitute nurse allow him to walk?

Around 7:00 p.m., two physicians who neither Jim nor my parents had seen before entered Jim's room and examined him. They learned that Jim was a smoker, and one of the physicians said that Jim looked like *"shit,"* which upset my mother greatly. They reconfirmed the diagnosis of a bacterial infection and said that Jim's condition was unchanged from the day before, even though oxygen alarms were sounding and he was spitting up blood.

Through the evening, the oxygen alarms kept sounding every so often, and Jim continued to cough up blood. At 2 a.m., my mother called the hospital to see how Jim was doing, and the nurse informed her Jim was not doing well. When my mother asked what else could be done, the nurse abruptly terminated the conversion.

The next afternoon — the last day of Jim's life — his face was puffy and swollen. He was exhausted because he had not slept for three days. And he was scared. Around mid-afternoon, tests were ordered to run a probe up his groin to see if anything had been missed around the heart. A nurse told my parents, *"We're finally going to do something for this young man! We're going to take action!"* My parents were shocked and thought to themselves, *"What do you mean you're going to finally do something? What have you people been doing for the last two days?"*

The test showed one major artery blocked 95% or better and three other arteries blocked 60% or better. Furthermore, one of his heart valves was completely destroyed Three physicians told my parents that surgery would be needed in the next day or so, but not to worry. The lead physician patted my mother's hand and said, *"Mother, don't worry, Jim will have a normal and healthy life . . . we fix people."*

However, a few minutes later, the three doctors rushed back to my parents and with hurried, excited voices informed them that Jim was crashing. The nurses were putting him on a ventilator and preparing him for surgery, and the doctors hustled my parents to see Jim. Mom and Dad saw Jim for a brief moment, during which Jim screamed not to let them put him on a machine. Those were his last words.

An hour later, the surgeon arrived at the hospital and spoke with my parents. To my parents' disbelief, the surgeon said he did not think Jim would make it off the operating table. He left to scrub in, and nurses escorted my parents to a waiting room. The nurses kept using the word *"grave"* to describe Jim's condition, and they insisted that Mom eat some high-calorie food so she could endure the *"long, terrible night ahead."*

A few hours later, the ER resident who had quipped about the *"art of medicine"* and had been part of the original team of physicians that diagnosed Jim with a bacterial infection informed my parents that Jim's ear lobes and fingertips were blue by the time he was put on the heart-lung machine. Unbelievably, the resident had a smile on his face when he delivered this news to them! He then abruptly halted the conversation, saying he had to run home to his three children. Unbelievable.

My parents were in a waiting room with their pastor and close friends. The nurses kept coming in every half or so to say the situation was very, very grave. My mother knew Jim was going to die. She felt very hot and flush and kept visiting the woman's bathroom to splash cold water on her face and lean against a cold wall; then she would return to the waiting room. On one return trip to the waiting room she bumped into the cardiologist who had diagnosed Jim with a bacterial infection of the heart. When the cardiologist saw my mother, his eyes widened and he immediately turned around and began walking quickly in the other direction and darted down another hall. My mother, who raised three boys and knows how to catch men, tracked him down. She demanded to know what had happened. The cardiologist began stumbling around, picking at his hands, and mumbling that the bacterial infection prevented surgery from happening sooner. But then why were they operating now if Jim still had a bacterial infection? The nervous, distraught doctor made no sense and only angered my mother further.

Less than two hours later, Jim was dead.

The surgeon, who had not been involved in Jim's care prior to the surgery, walked out of the operating room in surgical garb and told my father the following in a very angry tone: *"If the jerks at this hospital had done their job and gotten your son to me two days ago when they should have I could have saved him — no problem. We do bypass surgeries all the time, and your son would be on his way to recovery, but he is dead. I'm sorry."*

My father and the surgeon spoke extensively about the diagnosis of a bacterial infection, and the surgeon said the heart tissue had no signs of bacterial infection or his stitches would not have held. Furthermore, the surgeon was shocked by the treatment Jim had received. The surgeon suggested an autopsy.

The autopsy was performed, and no sign of bacterial infection was found. Official cause of death: Heart attack.

The same day the autopsy results arrived, we also received a sympathy card from the hospital addressed to Mrs. Jim Wojcieszak. Jim was not married.

After the funeral and all the relatives and friends went home, my parents went back to the hospital seeking answers, especially my father, the Ph.D. engineer. *"What happened? Why did it happen? Can the processes be improved so it never happens again?"* These were all questions my parents — especially my dad — had. But the door was unceremoniously slammed in their face. Meetings were promised, but did not transpire. Even the surgeon who was so honest the night Jim died told my parents: *"Look, our legal counsel has instructed me not speak with you any further. You will have to leave."*

Here was my father, who made a living asking countless questions and improving processes so aircraft engines and nuclear-powered naval vessels would be safe, being not-so-politely told to butt out of his own son's death. *"None of your business — get lost."* Maddening.

This deny-and-defend, circle-the-wagons routine made my parents extremely angry. It made litigation, which should have been the last recourse, the only option available to us. It made money, which should have been the third or fourth concern, the only issue worth fighting over. So, we filed a lawsuit.

I remember receiving calls from my parents any time our plaintiff's attorney called them. Getting a call from the lawyer's office was good — somebody was taking them seriously. Somebody cared. Somebody wanted to do something.

However, the defense depositions of my parents were a nightmare. At one point, my mother was crying so hard our attorney stopped the deposition, at which time one defense attorney turned to one of his colleagues and started chatting about his kid's soccer team. My father was furious at this callous behavior.

My parents described the overall litigation experience as a hellish episode of reliving their son's death every day for a year and a half. They thought the process was going to cause them to have heart attacks! Indeed, filing a lawsuit was not a "lottery ticket" or a game. They simply wanted answers, justice, and for the medical system to improve so the mistakes would not be repeated.

After a year and a half of litigation in Cincinnati (not a "judicial hellhole" by any stretch of the imagination), the judge literally turned to the hospital, doctors, and their attorneys and proclaimed they were wasting the court's time, malpractice was clear, and they should settle with our family.

At that point, the lawyers and insurers came up with the brilliant idea of offering our family a few thousand dollars, which angered the judge, and he demanded they make a good faith effort to settle the case before wasting any more of his time.

We received a sizeable settlement, which is sealed. After money exchanged hands and my parents signed the liability waiver, the *attorneys* — not the physicians — apologized, but no one ever admitted fault. Furthermore, no one ever took ownership of the mistakes, nor did they tell us how the hospital and doctors were going to improve their processes so the same mistakes would never be repeated.

Despite the fact our family received money — what tort reformers consider the holy grail of medical malpractice — we still have not found peace almost a decade after Jim's death. We are still angry with the doctors who have never sought us out and apologized, even though they have no further liability in our case (we cannot sue them anymore). Furthermore, we believe the errors that killed Jim are injuring and killing other patients today. Indeed, *maddening*.

That's my personal story that led to the development of Sorry Works! However, the creation of Sorry Works! also includes my professional life. I am a public relations and political consultant. I started my career working in the Illinois legislature on the Republican side of the aisle as a staff member. I worked on tort reform issues, and around the time my brother's case was being litigated, I was offered a job as the state-wide director of a pro-tort reform group aptly named "Illinois Lawsuit Abuse Watch." When I was interviewing for the job, I told the people on the other side of the table about Jim's case, and they universally replied, "*Oh, we believe in legitimate litigation, but it's the frivolous, wacky lawsuits that delay justice for good people like you and your family.*" They offered the job, and I accepted.

I started working for Illinois Lawsuit Abuse Watch – or I-LAW – in November 1999, and a month later the first scholarly paper on the benefits of disclosure and apology was published by Dr. Steve Kraman and Ginny Hamm, JD of the Lexington, Kentucky, Veterans Affairs (VA) Hospital.[1] In short, the paper said that the litigation experience at their hospital appeared to improve by disclosing, apologizing, and compensating patients and families after legitimate medical errors. That paper really spoke to me. It was common sense. So, I took the paper to my boss in the Illinois tort reform movement. I was convinced that this idea of disclosure could benefit the doctors, healthcare organizations, and insurers that funneled so much money into the tort reform movement — as well as patients and families.

My boss responded, "*Doug, we should never tell a doctor that he or she is wrong.*"

I was flabbergasted. "*You know my story…you know what happened to my brother,*" I rebutted. "*Of course doctors make mistakes…the question is are those mistakes going to be litigated or is there a better way? I believe this paper shows us a better way…it makes a lot of sense to me.*"

To which my boss replied, "*Well, Doug, you can take a trip down to the AMA or Illinois State Medical Society, but I can't guarantee you'll have a job when you get back.*"

I was 29 years old and living in Chicago with bills to pay, so I dropped the idea and got back to the tort reform hymnal of capping damages and beating up the plaintiff's bar. However, my eyes had been opened to the realities of medical malpractice politics.

I worked for I-LAW for a year and then went back to the Illinois legislature for a short stint, after which time I formed my own public relations firm. The plaintiff's bar in Illinois knew that I could talk about litigation issues, and they asked if I could tell their side of story in the Illinois medical malpractice debate. I said *"sure"* because they did have a story to tell. Through my PR firm, we talked about typical plaintiff concerns of increasing doctor discipline and reforming insurance companies; however, I revisited the disclosure issue. This time I had a chance to talk with Dr. Steve Kraman at the VA and other people involved in disclosure. My firm developed the term "Sorry Works!" to describe the process of apology and disclosure after medical errors, and we began attracting media coverage in Illinois. Some funny things started to happen.

Trial lawyers said Sorry Works! fit with how they were trained in law school to get justice for their clients. My clients told me that despite all the bad things said in the media about trial lawyers being greedy ambulance chasers, they were trained as advocates to always seek four things for patients and families: Answers, accountability, fixes, and swift justice. To them, Sorry Works! delivered in all four areas, and they encouraged our firm to continue forward.

However, we also started receiving calls from healthcare and insurance professionals, and the conversation on the other end of the line was always a little strained and awkward: *"Hey, Benedict Arnold, I mean, Doug, we know you traded us in for the trial lawyers, but this Sorry Works! stuff is really interesting. Where can we get some more information?"*

As a political professional I knew we were on to something.

> **"Sorry Works! is truly a middle-ground solution to the medical malpractice crisis… Fewer lawsuits and better control over liability exposure for healthcare and insurance professionals; swift justice with no constitutional limits for patients, families, and their attorneys; and safer healthcare, which benefits everyone."**

Sorry Works! is truly a middle-ground solution to the medical malpractice crisis. It is rare to find solutions to highly polarized debates that provide all sides what they want most, but this is exactly what Sorry Works! appeared to be able to do: Fewer lawsuits and better control over liability exposure for healthcare and insurance professionals; swift justice with no constitutional limits for patients, families, and their attorneys; and safer healthcare, which benefits everyone.

So, in February 2005, my PR firm helped organize The Sorry Works! Coalition as a nationwide group of healthcare, insurance, and legal professionals as well as patients, families, and consumers. I currently serve as the group's spokesperson.

As a reader you may say, *"Well, Wojcieszak, you have quite a story. I'm sorry to hear about your brother...don't like to hear about such tragic cases. And you certainly do have an interesting professional background having worked for both tort reformers **and** the trial bar, but nowhere in the last few pages did I read that you're a physician, lawyer, or insurance professional. You've never treated anyone, you've never defended a doctor or hospital against a lawsuit, nor have you had to write a claims check. So, if you've never walked in our shoes, how you can write anything in the pages to follow that is going to have any credibility or relevance to me? We in healthcare usually only take advice from our colleagues."*

Here's my perspective...I'm the patient...I'm the family member...I'm the *customer*, and the *customer* perspective is a critical issue in the medical malpractice crisis. Several major hospitals and insurers have figured out this simple fact, and by instituting a disclosure program they have significantly reduced lawsuits and litigation expenses. For example, the University of Michigan Health System (the largest hospital system in Michigan) has cut lawsuits in half, reduced litigation expenses by two-thirds (or $2 million annually), and reduced their insurance reserves from $72 million in 2001 to less than $20 million in 2007.[2] Similar positive figures about disclosure and apology programs are being reported by the University of Illinois Medical Center, Catholic Healthcare West, Kaiser Hospitals, the VA Hospitals, COPIC Insurance, and others. The Sorry Works! Coalition was created in 2005 to share these success stories and to encourage more hospitals, insurance companies, and providers to embrace disclosure and apology.

Further, in 2006, I made the connection with James Saxton of the law firm of Stevens & Lee. Jim is a trial lawyer by training and has spent over 25 years defending doctors and hospitals in the courtroom. He and the firm of Stevens & Lee have been at the forefront of helping to create insurance companies and advise physicians and hospitals on disclosure issues. I was surprised but pleased to hear Jim at a national program say that doctors must begin to move up the five-star curve and that enhanced communication post-disclosure was critical. It was clear to me that collaboration was key. Since then, we have spoken at the same programs and work together on cutting-edge programs and tools to make Sorry Works! work. In fact, this book is one of those collaborations.

Providers need to understand — and this book will teach — that people can actually live with mistakes, even serious mistakes, if the offending party is honest, candid, and quick to offer reasonable solutions. However, people cannot live with, accept, or tolerate cover-ups. This intolerance of cover-ups is amplified when it involves our health or the well-being of a loved one we entrusted to a medical professional.

"That doctor won't return my phone calls... the nurses won't look me in the eye... no one will give me answers or level with me... just what the hell is going on here?"

It is precisely this anger that pushes *customers* to call a lawyer. Remember, most folks do not like lawyers, so a *customer* has to be extremely angry to pick up the phone and call a lawyer. Also, remember this one simple truism: The most successful trial lawyer is powerless without an angry *customer* calling them. Trial lawyers do not have printing presses in the basements of their offices that churn out clients. No, *customers* have to call them.

Review Points:

- Patients and families — *customers* — are the drivers of the medical malpractice crisis, not lawyers.
- Anger causes patients and families to call a plaintiff's lawyer.
- An apology and disclosure program can benefit providers and patients.

CHAPTER 2
WHAT "I'M SORRY!" IS...AND IS NOT

Contemptible — Sad — Pitiful — Contrite — Pathetic. These are synonyms for "sorry."[3] Given the connotations of these words, it is no wonder that some healthcare providers are apprehensive in saying, *"I'm sorry."*

"Sorry" is defined by Merriam-Webster as:

1. "feeling sorrow, regret, or penitence"
2. "mournful, sad"
3. "inspiring sorrow, pity, scorn, or ridicule: pitiful"[4]

As with many words in the English language, the word "sorry" can have several meanings, and that is what can bring confusion to saying, "I'm sorry," in the context of healthcare. If a doctor says, "I'm sorry," and the patient interprets it as meaning, "I'm penitent and regret my misdeed," surely it is being misconstrued as an admission of fault, when it is not intended to be so.

In the context of communication with a patient and/or family post-adverse event, "I'm sorry" should not be construed as an admission of fault (except in very limited, specific circumstances). The key is putting "I'm sorry" into *context* post-adverse event. It is what you say after "I'm sorry" that places your statement in context to get you to the meaning of sorrow rather than a perception of an admission of fault.

Do not say:

"I'm sorry. It is all my fault."

"I'm sorry...if I just hadn't ...[you fill in the blank!]."

"I'm sorry. This is the first time I've ever done this procedure."

"I'm sorry I made such a mistake."

Do say:

"I'm sorry about this complication. Let's talk about what we think happened..."

"I'm sorry for your loss. I want to review what we know at this point..."

Saying "I'm sorry" should be an expression of empathy, sympathizing with your patient and/or patient's family. It should not typically be an expression of fault. It is important to separate these two concepts. There are times when admitting fault is appropriate and necessary. Fortunately, this is a small subset. Unfortunately, the trend of saying "I'm sorry" has led to confusion between an expression of sympathy and one of responsibility or an admission of fault. Many commentators have been pushing this concept of "I'm sorry" to necessarily require an admission of fault.

Admittedly the terminology can be confusing. Let's set the record straight!

Always express empathy post-adverse event.

"I'm sorry" is an expression of empathy.

An "apology" is a communication that also expresses responsibility.

Only apologize after due diligence has proven that a medical error occurred.

This is how these terms will be used throughout this book, and it is how the healthcare industry should perceive these terms in efforts to eliminate confusion. We need standardized language so that we can understand each other! Doing so is not new to healthcare. For example, in obstetrics, it was recognized that healthcare providers, nurses, obstetricians, etc., were attributing different meanings to words used to describe fetal heart tracing, and these differences in meanings could lead to misunderstandings and adverse events. The National Institute of Child Health and Human Development set forth standard terminology and definitions in efforts to have everyone speaking the same language. We need to do the same with "I'm sorry" and apology!

When an admission of fault is expressed, unfortunately, at times it has been expressed in the wrong types of cases. The key is to not always express fault, because that does have serious liability consequences (the ones that healthcare providers fear), but to express fault in the right circumstances.

However, we must always express empathy and communicate early and often post-adverse event.

Circumstances will exist that will require not only an expression of empathy, but also an admission of fault, an apology. However, this would only be after true due diligence and legal counsel should be consulted. In this narrow subset, it is essential to apologize and to accept responsibility in the right way so that you can reach the intended result of open communication, truthfulness, and preservation of the physician-patient relationship. This can lead to closure for the patient and family, as well as the physician. An appropriate example would be wrong site surgery, but there are others. Sometimes it is easy to determine whether responsibility should attach; at other times, it is not.

Too often, risks of a procedure or known complications are being perceived or misconstrued as a medical error. It is what makes the patient education and informed consent process so important. The right process will help prevent the jump to the conclusion that a medical error occurred when in fact a known complication, which was discussed pre-surgery with the patient, occurred. A good informed consent can be a significant aid to disclosure, and this will be reviewed in a future chapter.

"I'm sorry" shows respect and is a way of showing empathy. It may diffuse anger and prevent misunderstandings. It can also include acknowledging a complication, an adverse result, or a medical error. While "I'm sorry" cannot undo the harm incurred, it can prevent consequences from that harm. When it comes to healthcare, those consequences may include preventing a strained physician-patient relationship and preventing a claim or lawsuit. This is discussed in more detail in the next chapter. For our purposes here, the key is to understand that you should always express empathy post-adverse event, and whether you also apologize is dependent on the circumstances.

When considering whether an apology should be expressed post-adverse event, it is important to understand the differences among adverse events, complications, and medical errors. The lack of uniform definitions for these terms has caused confusion as well, and there are different meanings attributed to those terms by patients and physicians. The Institute of Medicine has defined "medical error" as a "failure of a planned action to be completed as intended or use of the wrong plan to achieve an aim" and defines "adverse event" as "serious injury or death resulting from medical management, not the underlying condition of the patient."[5] JCAHO uses the term "sentinel event," which comes closest to the term "medical error." These definitions just do not work for our purposes.

Understand that the overarching term for any unexpected result, bad outcome, or complication is "adverse event." Think of it is the whole universe of potential negative results from care. A "medical error" and a "complication" are subsets. An adverse event could be the result of a medical error or not. The terms are not synonymous.

Medical errors have significant liability consequences. An "error," in relevant part, is defined by Merriam-Webster as: "[A]n act or condition of ignorant or imprudent deviation from a code of behavior."[6] When a medical error occurs, it is necessarily negligence (care provided was below the accepted standard of care). However, to be liable for medical malpractice or negligence, not only must an act or omission by a healthcare provider fall below an accepted standard of care but also that deviation must have caused injury or harm.[7] Accordingly, when a medical error occurs, due diligence and consultation with risk management and/or legal counsel will be needed.

When a medical error occurs, you should, as mentioned above, express empathy to patients and/or family. We also know when it comes to medical errors that patients want to hear an apology.[8] A 2003 study showed that when it comes to medical errors, patients want:

1. Disclosure of the error
2. To understand what happened
3. To understand why the error happened
4. To know how the consequences of the error will be mitigated
5. To be assured recurrences will be prevented
6. Emotional support, including an apology[9]

Remember, an apology is acceptance of responsibility. You should be the one accepting responsibility, but only if it is your responsibility! Oftentimes errors are the result of systems issues,[10] or they may be the result of care provided by another healthcare provider. Proper coordination among healthcare providers, risk management, and counsel is key. If it is your fault, take responsibility, but consult your legal counsel because of the implications that your statement and/or wording could have, including insurance coverage issues. Further, risk management and/or counsel can help with language and wording so that the right message gets across to the patient and/or family in the appropriate way.

In contrast, you should not accept responsibility for a complication. A complication is a type of adverse event, and one that is a known risk of a surgical procedure or treatment. It is defined by Merriam Webster as "a secondary disease or condition that develops in the course of a primary disease or condition and arises either as a result of it or from independent causes."[11] A true complication is not a negligent medical error. Again, empathy or "I'm sorry" is absolutely appropriate and necessary in these circumstances, but an apology (acceptance of responsibility) is not.

It is important to note that other circumstances may arise that fall outside of any of these circles; that is, circumstances arise that are not an adverse event, a medical error, or a complication, but that may require empathy or acceptance of responsibility. Those areas come in the day-to-day activities of customer service, communication, and documentation, which are not associated with an adverse event. For example, it may be a billing issue, an issue with an appointment, or an issue with obtaining results of diagnostic testing. These circumstances require appropriate management as well, which should also include an expression of empathy and may or may not require an apology. It is these types of circumstances that set the stage if an adverse event (medical error or complication) does occur at some later time in the physician-patient relationship. The foundation has been laid and will help with any subsequent discussion and communications that may need to occur with the patient. If it was not, and you did not apologize for the failure to return a telephone call or for a rude staff person or whatever the service or communication issue was, the patient remembers, and it will often times not be you that the patient turns to when an error or complication occurs, but it will be her attorney!

Clarifying what type of circumstance your patient has experienced (a medical error, a complication, or a service issue) will dictate your approach:

- Complication — requires an expression of empathy.
- Medical error — requires an expression of empathy and an apology (when due diligence has established responsibility).
- Service or other risk management issue — requires an expression of empathy and in the right circumstances an apology (in context).

The bottom line here is that "I'm sorry" does not necessarily mean "I'm responsible" or "I'm negligent," and apologies accompanied by an acknowledgement of fault are appropriate in certain circumstances. The key is to recognize the difference and prepare an appropriate delivery. Sorry works 100% of the time when done right. Indicating that one is "sorry" in a heartfelt fashion will make every situation better. It may serve to help preserve the relationship so further communication can take place. It may keep the physician on the same side of the table as the patient...a key goal in post-adverse event strategies. It will make both the patient and physician feel better. The particulars on "how" to apologize under these circumstances are explored in more detail in chapter 6.

Review Points

- Say, "I'm sorry," with context for your listener.
- "I'm sorry" is an expression of empathy.
- An apology is an acceptance of responsibility or admission of fault.
- An appropriate approach can decrease liability risk, make the patient and physician feel better, and strengthen the physician-patient relationship.
- When a medical error occurs and responsibility has been determined, an apology is needed along with an expression of empathy.
- When a complication occurs, an expression of empathy is needed. No apology should be made.

CHAPTER 3
WHY IT WORKS

1. What causes a patient or family to visit a plaintiff's attorney?
2. What impacts whether or not a plaintiff's attorney takes on a case?
3. Why do jurors award large verdicts?

Although malpractice cases start with an unfortunate clinical outcome, that may well not be the driver. The short answer to all the questions posed above is an adverse event coupled with an aggravating circumstance. Most often, that aggravating circumstance involves miscommunication or a lack of communication. Hickson reported that poor communication is a primary factor leading patients to sue and has linked both communication lapses and patient complaints to professional liability claims.[12] Levinson has shown that certain physician communication behavior is associated with fewer malpractice claims.[13] Your attorney-authors see this play out in depositions and courtrooms all too often.

One study has shown that patients simply are more likely to sue when a physician does not disclose an error.[14] Patients and families will reach out to a lawyer in efforts to find out what happened when they do not get answers from their doctor. Chapter 8 of this book is devoted to this very topic — finding ways to encourage patients to seek out their doctor *first* to find out what happened instead of feeling the need to have a lawyer first. Once the patient and family get to the lawyer, poor communication, service lapses, perceived miscommunication, or worse may become an important factor in whether the plaintiff attorney ultimately decides to take on the case.

Medical malpractice plaintiff attorney Philip H. Corboy, Jr. has explained to the authors:

> "When deciding on whether to take on a plaintiff's medical
> malpractice case, we look for the right theme and a value.
> The theme is what we will show the jury, and we want to
> be able to demonstrate for the jury that by making our
> suggested award, it will be doing the right thing. Issues like
> failures of a healthcare provider to disclose a medical error, to

accept responsibility, to communicate simply and truthfully, and to show empathy are examples of important themes. They are also factors which add value to a claim. Jurors relate with patients and they get angry when doctors fail to admit mistakes. Patients have an inherent right to know about their treatment and when something goes wrong. Keeping information from the patient and his family only makes my case more valuable."[15]

It is not hard to understand that an aggravating circumstance in a case adds value. Value is clearly one factor plaintiff lawyers consider. They can use the lack of information or miscommunication in the courtroom, in front of a jury, who are peers of the patient and not the doctor. Poor communication and poor service can significantly impact a jury's decision on both liability and the size of the award. So-called courtroom drama is used by plaintiff attorneys to make a connection with the patient-jurors so that they relate to what the patient-plaintiff has gone through.[16] At times, jurors perceive a "cover-up" because there has been miscommunication, which also has a major impact on the verdict. Of course, the opposite works as well. If the communication was clear and compassionate it could be very helpful. The key is to recognize that post-adverse event communication is evidence...it is all evidence. The question will be is it positive or negative, and you, to a great extent, are in control of that.

We know that patients want to hear, "I'm sorry," after an adverse event.[17] It stands to reason that if you give the patients what they want — effective communication including an understanding of what happened, why it happened, the medical consequences, how recurrence will be prevented, and empathy — then you may well prevent your patient from visiting a lawyer in the first place. If for some reason, the patient does visit a lawyer, the aggravating circumstance that may impact the lawyer's evaluation and willingness to accept the case would not be present.

This effective communication is part of customer or patient service. One could argue that the medical malpractice crisis, in part, is a *customer* service crisis that has been miscast as a legal one to be solved by politicians. In other words, the medical malpractice crisis is a *customer* service problem that can be fixed by healthcare and insurance professionals. You cannot wait for the government or politicians to fix it. You do not have to convince politicians to cast a vote or have judges issue favorable rulings because you can implement an excellent *customer* service program whenever you want, and it can never be taken away. This book provides the framework to do so.

Studies have supported this concept for over a decade that anger — not greed — is what drives most *customers* to file medical malpractice lawsuits. This is not a new revelation. Dr. Gerald Hickson of Vanderbilt University Medical School, as noted above, and many other researchers have published numerous papers in peer-reviewed medical journals stating this very fact: Anger from poor communication is the key driver of medical malpractice lawsuits. There is the potential to reduce the potential of a claim and value of a claim by embracing this concept. Doctors and insurance companies have fought for appropriate tort reform, which should continue, but that is treating the symptoms of the problem and not the root cause of it: Anger. Disclosure, enhanced communication, and a stronger physician/patient relationship goes to the heart of this issue.

> **"It has actually been known and understood for over a decade that anger — not greed — is what drives most *customers* to file medical malpractice lawsuits."**

Accordingly, if we reduce patient anger, we can reduce the number of lawsuits filed and achieve other benefits, including decreased litigation costs, reduction in medical errors, better public relations, and physician benefits. While this may not be new information, new *energy* is needed!

An astute doctor or insurance professional might rebut, *"But you know there are some patients who only want to get money when things go wrong. It's become a lottery!"* It is true; there are some greedy people, but the *majority* of people who enter healthcare facilities every day, be they practitioners or customers, are there for the right reasons. Patients and families want healing, and medical providers want to heal. However, adverse events (with and without error) do occur, despite the best of intentions. Medicine is not perfect, but deny-and-defend risk-management practices turn good people into bitter enemies. Deny and defend produces anger and then litigation. This book provides a constructive, pro-active methodology to keep healthcare professionals and their customers working together, maintaining relationships, and solving problems...on the same side of the table, without heading to the courtroom.

Remaining on the same side of the table is optimal for all.

Eliminate anger and most lawsuits will be eliminated. It is just that simple. Do not forget about the other benefits too:

- Defense litigation expenses reduced
  Defense litigation expenses are a major cost factor for medical professional liability insurance carriers and self-insured hospitals and are often cited as a major reason for the spike in medical professional liability insurance premiums over the last several years. If you review an insurance company's closed claims, you will find that defense litigation expenses often dwarf settlement costs. With empathy, apology, and disclosure, defense litigation expenses can be reduced dramatically. The University of Michigan Health System has reported a dramatic reduction in their defense litigation costs of $2 million annually, or two-thirds, because of their disclosure and transparency program. One of the reasons for

the reduction is that cases are resolved earlier, in a matter of months rather than years through the court system. Further, depositions, discovery, motions, and court appearances are largely eliminated from the expense budget for the claim. Even if a lawsuit is initiated after disclosure and an attempt to compensate, the scope of the litigation can be reduced to focus on damages, which also has a beneficial impact on defense litigation expenses. On the flip side, cases where no error occurred are less likely to see a nonmeritorious lawsuit filed (more directly below).

- Nonmeritorious litigation reduced
Nonmeritorious medical malpractice lawsuits account for 60 percent to 80 percent of all medical malpractice lawsuits filed in the United States.

  When healthcare providers cut off communication after adverse events, patients perceive a lack of caring or even a cover-up — even if they did not commit an error! Again, this is when they seek out a lawyer. The lawyer hears the patient's side of the story, obtains the medical records, and obtains an expert review to determine whether a case exists. Sometimes, information needed to determine liability cannot be gleaned from the records, and the lawyer will need to name nurses, doctors, and the hospital in a case and take discovery and depositions to determine if there was an error and/or who was at fault. You can prevent this scenario by enhancing communication post-adverse event with empathy, apology, and disclosure. Not only is communication post-adverse event your opportunity to explain what, how, and why something went wrong, but also why everything went right (why no fault exists even if there was an adverse event or a perceived adverse event).

- Errors reduced
Under a deny-and-defend strategy, mistakes are buried and generally not learned from. You wonder how many

healthcare professionals hear their high school history teachers ringing in their ears: *"Those who fail to learn from history are doomed to repeat the mistakes of the past!"* How true.

With a disclosure program supported by an event management program, mistakes, near misses, and errors are discussed openly and treated as golden learning opportunities. It is a living, learning laboratory. Use the adverse events as an opportunity to prevent future, similar events from occurring. We know patients want reassurance that the event will not recur. Do a root cause analysis, institute remedial measures, and educate staff and physicians. When errors are reduced, so is the liability exposure.

- Better public relations
  Healthcare facilities in the United States spend enormous sums of money promoting their services.

  "We're the heart hospital...the best place to deliver your baby...cure your cancer...mend your kid's broken leg...etc., etc."

  You cannot open a newspaper or turn on the television without being pelted by multiple advertisements from a local hospital claiming to be "Top 100." It is understandable, because healthcare facilities and providers are businesses and business people — they need customers to walk through the front door to keep the lights on. However, how much money is being lost from bad publicity generated by a deny-and-defend strategy or lawsuits that are in court but do not belong there? Angry customers not only tell sad tales to their attorneys, but they also vent to family, friends, neighbors, the lady on the bus, the mailman, and other any other sympathetic ear.

  "That hospital is nothing more than a Band-aid station. You won't believe what they did to my husband Frank. I am going to own that damn hospital by the time me and my lawyer are done!'

This is the kind of bad publicity that drives patients away and can eventually destroy the bottom line of an institution. Word of mouth is one of the strongest advertisements.

However, with a disclosure program, you can draw patients and families closer after an adverse event with good customer service techniques. You can also save relationships. The Lexington VA Hospital reports story after story of patients and families coming back to their facility after an error, even when they had other healthcare choices. Why did this happen? Simple: The facility and professionals had enough character to own up to their mistakes and fix the problems they created. Patients and families respect and admire that kind of character in an institution.

Healthcare professionals invest a lot of money and time building relationships. An adverse event does not mean that investment has to be lost.

- Saving the medical staff
  Medical errors produce three victims: The patient, the family, and the healthcare providers. The popular media, the trial bar, and politicians focus almost exclusively on the pain and suffering experienced by patients and families (and their pain is very real), but almost no one discusses the trauma visited upon healthcare professionals after errors. Doctors and nurses literally suffer in silence.

  A jaded consumer advocate might rebut, *"Fine, who cares?! Let the sloppy doctor or nurse suffer. Serves them right!"*

  But disclosure is truly about reconciliation and solving problems for all sides in the medical malpractice debate, and the situation described herein is a real problem. Adverse events (with and without error) literally tear up good doctors and nurses. Healthcare professionals are talented and caring people who take pride in what they do. A mistake does not make them a bad person worthy of scorn and condemnation.

There are countless sad cases of healthcare professionals experiencing clinical depression, ruined practices and careers, divorces and broken families, and even suicides after medical errors.

Tort reform is not going to help doctors heal. If, however, healthcare and insurance professionals accept that anger — not greed — is the driver of medical malpractice, then support mechanisms for providers who have made mistakes can be included in the development of disclosure programs. Providers need support after disclosure from their colleagues and institutions. Furthermore, doctors and nurses need to be given the chance to look patients and families in the eye and say, *"I'm sorry,"* and hear back, *"We forgive you."* Indeed, confession is good for the soul. It is all about healing.

Recognizing the cause of frequency and severity of medical malpractice claims means that we can now provide a communication framework for reducing liability risk associated with poor communication. Anger is the ball we must keep our eyes on. A proactive and aggressive customer service program that mitigates anger, reduces litigation and associated expenses, provides healing for all sides, and increases patient safety is the key. Also, remembering that this post-adverse event activity is evidence upon which the circumstance will be judged is important too. Done well, a claim can be prevented, positive evidence created, but most importantly, a relationship preserved.

Review Points:

- An adverse event coupled with an aggravating circumstance (poor communication or miscommunication, service lapse) is the driver of frequency and severity.
- Controlling and mitigating anger felt by patients and families after adverse events is the key to reducing lawsuits and settlement costs. Anger — not greed — is the key factor!

- An effective disclosure program can reduce causes of litigation with additional benefits for the patient, physicians, and healthcare organization.
- Attack the medical liability problem with risk management strategies for prevention, rather than just treating the symptoms.

CHAPTER 4

EVENT MANAGEMENT PROCESS: THE PLATFORM FOR A DISCLOSURE PROGRAM

As set forth in the previous chapter, the reasons empathy, apology, and disclosure work are really twofold: (1) Strengthening the physician-patient relationship by providing answers to the patient and/or family and thereby diffusing anger and (2) Creating the appropriate evidence to be used for you instead of against you. While many healthcare providers and organizations can get on-board with the concept, they always ask, now what? How do we do this? How do we make it practical? How do we make sure apology and disclosure happen? How do we make sure apology and disclosure occur in the right circumstances? How do we make sure apology and disclosure are done the right way?

The answer is to first implement an apology and disclosure infrastructure in your organization that will support this post-adverse event communication. How to implement a disclosure program is discussed in the next chapter, followed by literally how to apologize and disclose. This chapter focuses on "event management," which is the foundation to support your disclosure program.

What is it?

People often ask, "What do you mean by 'event management'? If you mean throwing a party, I like parties!" Event management is not about throwing a party; it is a process where support can be given after an adverse event occurs in an effort to ensure that good communication and appropriate documentation occur and that patients and families are kept informed. It is about coordination and collaboration between healthcare professionals for the benefit of patients. Event management is what will support your apology and disclosure program. It may mean having a meeting with a patient and/or family to discuss the patient care so that questions can be asked and answered; it may mean coordinating the information coming from different providers so the patient and family receive a clear message; and it may mean following up with them and being a continued resource for tough questions (*"What about the bills? Did someone do something wrong?"*). Every circumstance will be different and may need to be managed differently. In some circumstances, an apology may be needed. On other occasions it can be diffusing the angry patient who has suffered a known complication of a procedure. When any of those circumstances arise, having in place an event management program will help the process move forward in a methodical and organized fashion.

What are the benefits?

A true event management program will help in your efforts to reduce liability risk, but it has other benefits as well. While in the first instance, an event management program addresses the immediate event — managing the communication issues — it also provides a means for a living, learning laboratory or continuous quality improvement: Could we have done something differently to have prevented the outcome? Can we incorporate a tool or strategy to reduce future similar events? This quality assurance aspect of event management can lead to reduced medical errors and increased patient satisfaction. Doing so affects the two factors that cause claims: (1) The injury or clinical circumstance and (2) The aggravating circumstance. Therefore, you get to positive risk reduction.

"We have found a strong association between patient satisfaction and risk management," says Dr. Melvin Hall, President and CEO of Press Ganey Associates, Inc. "Those providers who excel in providing patient-centered care — from communication to involving patients in treatment decisions to treating patients with dignity — reduce the likelihood of litigation. Bottom line — satisfied patients are less likely to sue."[18] Press Ganey has found that a one-point decrease in a practice's satisfaction score is associated with a 5% increase in the rate of risk management episodes. Press Ganey is the nation's leading provider of health care performance improvement services.

There is a direct correlation between employee satisfaction and patient satisfaction. Increasing employee satisfaction bolsters productivity and staff retention. "There is a strong demonstrated relationship between an organization's patient satisfaction and the satisfaction among the organization's employees," says Dr. Hall. "Health care organizations that focus on the needs of their employees find staff members are able to more fully engage in their roles and better focus on providing high quality care. Improving the quality of care and 'making a difference' is the reason most professionals enter the health care field."[19]

Benefits of a true event management program include other positives for the physicians, hospital, counsel, and, most importantly, the patient. For the patient, it can lead to improved care, improved safety, and a stronger physician-patient relationship. For physicians and other healthcare providers, the relationship with the patient is maintained and can also result in decreased liability risk. The risk reduction benefit also comes from the evidence created in the process. This benefits the healthcare provider and the defense counsel, who has evidence, perhaps evidence he or she would not have had before, to defend the client's case. That evidence may be a note in a medical chart pertaining to a discussion with a patient and/or family about the complication that occurred, which acknowledges the patient's understanding of the same, for example.

Any event management program should address confidentiality issues. By this, we do not mean physician-patient confidentiality, but we do mean confidentiality of the investigation process and communications between the physicians, hospital, and counsel. Event management is most effective when it can be done in a framework of this type of confidentiality. This helps to allow for a more open communication and analysis to truly to get the root cause. It also provides you with the ability to control the information. Programs exist where this is accomplished through collaboration with legal counsel.

In summary, benefits of a true event management program include:

- Decreasing professional liability risk
- Decreasing claims and lawsuits
- Creating positive evidence if you are sued
- Decreasing medical errors — continuous quality improvement
- Increasing patient satisfaction
- Strengthening the physician-patient relationship
- Enhancing your bottom line
- Increasing staff retention
- Becoming the employer of choice
- Becoming the provider of choice
- Peer-review/attorney-client privilege protections

How do you accomplish it?

With all of the positive benefits associated with event management, what can you do to ensure an effective event management program exists? Incorporate an event management policy, educate your physicians and staff on the policy, and follow it! Policies are important whether you are a hospital or a physician-office practice, because they provide a standardized and consistent process for handling difficult circumstances. They also serve to provide employees and staff with direction and can be the basis for support. Use policies also to orient new employees or physicians. Perhaps one of the most important benefits is the ability to create potential evidence for claim resolution if necessary. This is where the confidentiality protections become essential.

How do you ensure that your policy is followed? Provide education and training to your physicians and staff. You can hold organization-wide educational programming for staff and a separate program for physicians. Outside speakers could be brought in who can describe event management and show its benefits. To reinforce the policy, provide in-services and annual educational programs.

One of the best methods for bringing physicians and staff on-board is to create a collaborative event management program. By collaborative, we mean that it transcends the hospital and the physician's practice. One area your attorney authors have worked extensively with this concept is in obstetrics. For example, coordinate and collaborate with the obstetricians, pediatricians, neonatologists, labor hall, anesthesia, and nurses. Event management facilitators are provided extra training and provide support as events occur. Such an event management program brings everyone on-board with the concept.

What needs to be done when an event actually occurs?

Perhaps you now have an event management policy, you have had education, but what do you do when an event actually occurs?

1. Ensure that the patient is safe and ensure that an appropriate treatment plan in response to the event is formulated and in place. This should be the initial primary concern.
2. Follow your event management policy and notify the proper individuals. For example, you may need to notify hospital risk management, and you may need to notify your insurance company as

well. Notice to your insurance carrier could impact coverage for any event or claim. Notify your insurer promptly, consistent with your insurance carrier's mandates. Some innovative insurance companies require notification of events within a certain time period and will provide event management support.

3. Initially, ensure that the patient and/or family has a response to the pending issue. Often, you will only have initial information, and more investigation will be needed, letting the patient know candidly that this is part of the process. When no contact occurs, remember, they will seek out their attorney to get answers if too much time passes.

4. Gather information so that you can provide it to your risk management and/or insurance company, who can provide you with support. For example, what happened, what were the discussions pre-event with the patient, what is documented in the medical record? Specifically, as an example, if a known complication occurred, what did you discuss with the patient about the risks of the procedure? Was it you who had the discussion or someone else? Is it documented that the patient understood these risks? What discussions were had with the patient after the complication occurred? What is documented in the medical record about those conversations? As you can see, we are essentially gathering the *evidence* that will support (or not) your care.

5. Review the care. In an objective fashion, review your care. It is important to remember that this should not be done with the retroscope. It is always easier after the fact to say, "*I could have...; I wish I had...; I should have...*" However, you need to review the care as if it were contemporaneous with the facts known at the time treatment and care decisions were made and provided, not in retrospect with new facts and knowing the outcome of the care.

6. Collaboration among providers, risk management, and perhaps legal counsel may be needed. Get in the same room or on the telephone and discuss the circumstances of the event and make sure everyone is on the same page. Iron out issues among yourselves and not in front of the patient/family. This is not the time to place blame. Be respectful of one another. You will also need to collaborate on who takes the lead in discussions with the patient/family; who will be at the meeting or

discussion; who will document the meeting or discussion; who will be the contact after the patient/family meeting or discussion.

7. Collaboration in significant events involving many providers can be difficult. Every physician has an insurer. Every physician will have counsel. You could get together in a conference room and have three healthcare providers (the attending physician, the cardiologist, and anesthesia), two nurses (that were in the operating room), a risk manager, and four defense counsel (each of the providers may have counsel and the hospital may as well). However, it is in these types of circumstances that collaboration is essential. You can see how easily misinformation or conflicting information could get to the patient/family if collaboration does not occur. We are not saying to provide untruthful information, but we are saying, get to the facts and ensure that everyone is on the same page.

8. Leave this collaborative endeavor with a plan. Include discussions about what and how information will be relayed to the patient/family. You may need to practice with your counsel. For example, *"Mrs. Smith, I have met with the other healthcare providers that have been involved with your care since your admission here at Sacred Heart Hospital. We reviewed your care, including the medical records. We also had an independent, objective third-party cardiologist review your records. We are very sorry that you incurred one of those risks of the procedure that we discussed before your surgery. However, we do have a treatment plan that has been discussed among your physician team members. Here's what we are going to do..."* This does not necessarily come easy, especially when you are emotionally involved in a situation. Practice.

9. In determining who is best suited to communicate with the patient and/or family, most often it will be the provider, but consideration should be made of both the relationship with the patient and the communication skills of the provider. Sometimes the provider may not be the best-suited individual. Alternatives could include a nurse with a good relationship with the patient or even another physician.

10. Investigate, as necessary, following your event management policy, which may include interviewing witnesses, obtaining incident reports, and having the medical records reviewed by an expert. These types of things will be done by the individual at your facility that is responsible

for event management — it may be the risk manager, a patient safety officer, or a department head. You should not be the one literally interviewing other witnesses. This only places you at risk of being deposed at a deposition if a claim should result and you are not named as a defendant!

11. After any meeting or discussion with the patient/family, document it in the medical chart. Include who was present, a summary of the conversation/meeting, the time, the date, the location, the patient/family's understanding of what occurred and the next steps, and what the next steps are. For example, "*On February 22, 2007, at 12:11, in her hospital room, I met with Mrs. Smith to discuss the stroke she incurred following a cardiac catheterization that was performed this morning. We discussed her treatment plan of rehab and admission to a rehab facility, which she was in agreement with. I also discussed with her the fact that the stroke was a potential complication that we had discussed prior to the surgery. She recalled that discussion. She will be discharged to rehab, and I will follow her there.*"

12. All conversations with patient and/or family should be documented, *objectively*. Documentation should be limited to the facts and should not include emotions. If your organization requires that an incident report be completed, do so, but again, only provide objective facts. Oftentimes incident reports are discoverable should litigation ensue.

13. After any meeting, provide the patient and/or family with contact information for a point person should any questions arise after the initial discussion or communication. It can simply be that you provide them with one of your business cards. Include on the back your cell phone number or an alternative method of reaching you if you are not available at the number listed on the business card.

14. Follow up with the patient and/or family! So often we see this step falling through the cracks. Physicians and facilities do a great job of initially talking with the patient and even investigating what occurred, but then fail to circle back to the family. They are then surprised when they receive a records request from an attorney, and now it is just too late. You can schedule a face-to-face meeting, or if a telephone call is all that is needed you can do that as well; or perhaps it is a letter. Oftentimes, a face-to-face meeting would be most beneficial.

For example, perhaps you were waiting for the results of an autopsy report to discuss the cause of death with a family. Once the autopsy report results are in, call the family and schedule a meeting. At the meeting, you can show them the autopsy report and, importantly, explain what it means. *"The medical examiner has listed the cause of death as a pulmonary embolism. A pulmonary embolism occurs when clots break loose from the vein surface and block pulmonary blood vessels. Primary symptoms are chest pain and shortness of breath, which your son did not have. Sometimes pulmonary embolisms do not exhibit any symptoms, as occurred here. A pulmonary embolism is a risk of the gastric-bypass procedure performed, and a risk that we discussed with your son prior to his agreeing to move forward with surgery. Unfortunately, he experienced one of those risks, and we are very sorry for your loss. I would be happy to answer any questions you may have about this report or the care of your son. Do you have any questions? Perhaps you will have some after you leave and this new information settles in. Please call me if you have questions after you leave here today and I would be happy to discuss them with you.*

15. While the exact mechanics of "disclosure" are discussed in chapter 6, any time you speak with a family and/or patient after an adverse event, you need to expect that they will be anxious, nervous, and upset. They do not know what happened! You will also be nervous and upset, but you need to be a calming force — they are looking to you!

16. Keep the lines of communication open with the patient/family. Make yourself available and make sure they know how to reach you. You can touch base with them. A balance does exist though. You do not want to harass them.

17. Do not speak to other colleagues, your family, or your friends about the event. Your discussions about the event should only take place in the context of the event management policy (with the patient, the patient's family, the risk manager, counsel, or others). Otherwise, going outside these parameters could cause your colleagues, family, and friends to be deposed if you are named in a suit! They will not be very happy with you!

18. Ensure that systems are in place and followed to prevent reoccurrence. This should be done within your organizational systems. Perhaps

there is a patient safety officer in charge of this, or a committee or risk manager. If you are a physician in a physician practice, work with your office manager to implement new strategies, tools, and/or processes. For example, you may have a patient who incurred a pneumothorax after receiving a trigger point injection. Your office hears from a lawyer who wants the patient to be compensated for a hospitalization, pain and suffering, and time off work. The patient's attorney alleges that a pneumothorax is a known risk of a trigger point injection. Your office agrees to pay to help the patient. Your attorney tells you if the patient had signed an informed consent form that noted that a pneumothorax is a known risk, you probably would not have had to make any payment. The data and literature indicate that it is a known risk. Internally, you can create and implement a procedure-specific informed consent form for trigger point injections, which also sets forth the known risks of the procedure (including a pneumothorax). Next time a pneumothorax does occur as a result of a trigger point injection, and you discussed that risk with the patient, who has signed a procedure-specific form, you will be able to explain to the patient that it is a known risk of the complication, you discussed it previously, and remember the informed consent form that was signed.

How is disclosure a part of it?

As you can see, event management can provide you with appropriate evidence to be used for you through documentation and communication. What you say to the patient, how you say it, and what you document will affect whether all the benefits of event management are attained. Empathy, apology, and disclosure are forms of communication. (In chapter 6, details of the communication aspect of disclosure are addressed.) True event management is the shell that allows for disclosure, or effective communication, to take place. With an event management infrastructure in place, you are ready to incorporate an apology and disclosure program, which is supported by this infrastructure.

Review Points:

- A true event management policy and program are needed to support your apology and disclosure program.

- A true event management program is a process where support can be given after an adverse event occurs in an effort to ensure that good communication and appropriate documentation occur and that patients and families are kept informed.
- Implement (or update) an event management policy.
- An appropriate event management policy, if consistently followed, is beneficial in increasing patient satisfaction, increasing patient safety, providing continuous quality improvement, strengthening the provider-patient relationship, decreasing liability risk, and importantly to this book, providing the framework to support an apology and disclosure program, which comes with its added benefits.

CHAPTER 5

HOW TO IMPLEMENT A SORRY WORKS!
PROGRAM IN FIVE STEPS

Apology and disclosure are more than a policy — they are a program. Many healthcare institutions across the United States have adopted disclosure policies in the wake of the 2001 JCAHO standard on disclosure,[20] but few organizations have actual disclosure programs in place. Policies are fine, and are needed, but they are only part of the equation. Policies do not make disclosure happen. Programs do, with the combination of a disclosure program and an existing event management program.

For healthcare and/or insurance organizations to experience disclosure success stories similar to the University of Michigan (and elsewhere), a disclosure *program* has to be implemented. Such programs need the buy-in and support from the leadership of the hospital, physicians, and insurer(s) as well as the legal and risk management staff. Everyone has to be on the same page and committed to making the program a success. In fact, in our experience, for the program to work, there needs to be a champion who can start the process of putting a program in place.

There is nothing ad hoc about disclosure. The disclosure program should be consistently and uniformly applied to all adverse events, whether perceived as small or large in value, be they known or unknown to the patient and family. Successful disclosure programs involve consistent and constant high ethical standards. Consistent ethics translate into credible disclosure programs. Patients and families - the *customers* - and their attorneys, when involved, must feel they are receiving the whole truth at all times.

The program must also include training and tools as well as support in how to keep the process going so it can take hold. Just going to a seminar is a start, but it does not itself facilitate the change that needs to take place. The program structure must assure that appropriate, effective disclosure takes place consistently.

Consider the following five steps as you implement your disclosure program:

Step 1: Sorry Works! Starts With a Few Committed People — Get the Decision Makers On-Board!

Developing a disclosure program begins with you! Be the champion! Disclosure programs begin with a few "champions" who carry the flag and get the rest of the institution excited. They use the powerful data and combination of easily definable benefits of appropriate disclosure to bring the management on board (see chapter 9 for disclosure success stories). Disclosure not only makes economic sense, but it is also in keeping with most healthcare organizations' and physicians' values and culture.

Your job is to be the voice for disclosure. Be the champion, the example, as often it takes someone willing to push for a cause. People like to join in causes where enthusiasm is pervasive. You need to drive the concept and ultimately its success. It may actually be YOU who gets the concept into a program at your institution. YOU may be the one to handle the typical questions and challenges to disclosure (see Questions and Challenges at the end of this book). It may be YOU who pushes the next steps to obtain the organizational commitment. It will also then be YOU who will get the quiet sense of accomplishment when it happens and helps so many patients and medical staff members.

Leadership

Obtaining the commitment and buy-in from the leadership may be the single most important action that can lead to a successful disclosure program. If your leadership is not on-board, your program will never work.

In order to obtain this necessary buy-in, education is key. Educate the key leadership — the hospital CEO, board president, hospital risk manager, patient safety officer, and in-house counsel. Educational programs are available. The concept of disclosure and its *benefits* must be conveyed and understood. Further, they must understand that commitment is required, and more — training for the physicians and staff. It is not simply getting behind the concept of disclosure, but actually making it work, and that requires adequate training and education for those on the front lines. To be effective, disclosure must be done in the right way.

You can also incorporate conference calls with key disclosure and patient safety leaders who can answer any questions that the leadership may have. We have seen naysayers become supporters! It is just a matter of education.

You might hear from your leadership... *"Our staff and physicians do not want this."* It may be because doctors do not understand what "it" is. Discuss disclosure with your doctors. Your leadership and you may be surprised to find very receptive ears. The fact is that many healthcare professionals are tired of being told to run away or hide from patients and families after adverse events. Providers are also tired of trying to convince politicians to fix their liability problems. Disclosure offers providers the chance to begin to address their liability problems on their own, which is refreshing and different.

Eliminate the appearance of avoidance.

Committee

Create a committee to move the concept forward to reality. The committee is often comprised of physicians, nurses, risk managers, attorneys, and administrators who help develop the disclosure program. The committee will develop a policy and procedure, as outlined below, and importantly, ensure not only that the disclosure program occurs, but also that once it does, the program is kept alive! In part, this is done by incorporating a workable policy and program and making sure an education process takes place.

Some members of the steering committee could later form the nucleus of the disclosure team that leads the program, helps assure continued education, and helps determine who is going to be on the disclosure team.

Legal Counsel

Use your committee to obtain the buy-in of defense counsel. Oftentimes, the defense counsel's initial reaction to disclosure may be reluctance. You need to educate your defense counsel that in fact your disclosure program will help them! By disclosing in the right way, you actually can create favorable, appropriate evidence that will help your defense counsel should a case be pursued. Truly, most defense counsel at this point in time know that enhanced communication post-adverse event is the only option. Disclosure programs include enhanced communication and a whole lot more.

Insurer

As with the defense counsel, use your committee to obtain the buy-in of your insurer. In the present day, most hospitals are self-insured, so this happens through your risk manager, but if not, involve your insurer early, including insurer(s) that cover independent contractor physicians. When it comes to disclosure and apology programs, oftentimes insurers believe that the insured (doctors, hospitals) are not in favor of disclosure, and the insureds believe that the insurer will be opposed to disclosure. Sometimes that is the case, but you need to find out!

"As an insurance company, we think disclosure has a lot of promise. It certainly would seem to help our bottom line, but our doctors will never go for it. The 'a word' is not in their vocabulary."

"As a doctor, I think Sorry Works! is good for my patients and me, but the insurance company will say no. There's no way they'll go for this disclosure stuff. Insurance companies always say no to innovative ideas."

Everyone is in their silo, assuming that the other side will automatically say no. Doctors and hospital administrators can get this started. It only takes a phone call or an e-mail to their insurance carrier(s) with a question: *"Would you support implementation of a program that can increase patient safety and satisfaction at the same time that it can reduce professional liability risk?"* They might be surprised to learn that their insurance company is already studying the issue (chiefly because of the potential cost savings), and receiving support from their insureds will help. If the insurance company is not studying Sorry Works! or flat out says "no," then physicians and administrators need to realize that they are the customers and should demand that a disclosure program be incorporated and that they help. Write letters, send e-mails, make phone calls. If phone calls, letters, and protests do not work, you may need to look for a new insurer. It is your practice... your hospital... your patients... your liability problem... take control! Done the right way, and that is our whole point, there is very little downside.

Make no mistake, Sorry Works! is a culture change, and changing culture is never easy. We are asking healthcare and insurance organizations to shift from deny and defend to openness, honesty, and transparency. Some people will not like the change. Some individuals will resist, but the benefits are worth it.

Action Steps:
- Be the champion of disclosure
- Obtain the buy-in of your leadership — provide an educational program
- Obtain commitment from the decision makers (leadership, insurers, and in-house counsel)
- Identify other disclosure champions and form a disclosure committee
- Create your disclosure committee

Step 2: Adopt a Disclosure Policy and Procedure

It is important for the policy and procedure to be in place before you move forward with announcing the commitment to disclosure to the entire organization. You can find disclosure policies adopted by organizations by simply "Googling" the Internet (for example, the Veteran's Administration Directive or the University of Michigan). However, any one policy may not be the best fit for every organization. It is important to tailor a policy to suit your facility's needs and requirements and that it is consistent with your other policies that are in place. You may need to do some hard work when drafting your policy. While disclosure may seem like an easy issue, there are legal and risk implications and language and definition challenges. This is exactly what your committee can work through. ASHRM has provided some guidance.[21]

You need to recognize that any policy that is created may end up being evidence in litigation. Many states throughout the nation recognize a corporate negligence theory of liability against hospitals, and that can be based on whether you have a policy, and if you have one, if it is followed. The policy may be requested in the discovery process of litigation. You therefore need to ensure that your policy does the job it is intended to do — provide guidance for your healthcare providers — but at the same time, it is drafted in a way that is less likely to be used against your healthcare providers and/or the facility. When drafting a policy, consider the following:

1. <u>A statement on the purpose of the policy.</u> What is the purpose of your policy? Is it to increase patient safety, provide open communication with patients and their families, ensure that patients are kept informed of their health status, and/or provide guidelines to support your healthcare providers?

   Your disclosure policy's purpose could be:

   It is the goal of [insert name of institution or practice] to involve patients in their care and treatment through effective communication. This policy is intended to provide guidelines for disclosing certain adverse events to patients and/or their families.

2. <u>What "events'" are covered by the policy?</u> It is important to analyze and consider what your disclosure policy will cover. Will it include complications? Will it include near misses? You need to have agreement on this before rolling it out to your staff.

3. <u>Defining terms.</u> Much confusion in this area of disclosure has also presented due to varying nomenclature and the varying definitions that are attributed to those terms. For example, near miss, anticipated outcome, bad outcome, unanticipated outcome, adverse event, medical error, and so on. It's confusing!

4. <u>A policy statement.</u> You will need a policy statement, which should consider the subject matter of the policy and embrace its goals and the goals of the organization. Your policy statement may be:

Our [insert facility] is committed to providing the highest-quality and safest medical care to our patients. Patients must be treated with openness and honesty at all times, and their right to know their medical status must be respected. Patients will be provided with timely and accurate information with respect to outcomes of care, including adverse events, whether anticipated or unanticipated, and our healthcare providers will provide information with regard to medical errors with clinical consequences or when a reasonable person would want to know, whether or not there was a negative clinical consequence (a near miss).

5. How much guidance you want to provide. How much detail are you going to provide? Will you include actual sample language to use in discussions with family, for example, or are you going to provide general guidance and provide other resources?

6. "Who" the policy applies to. Does it apply to all healthcare providers?

7. "What" events must be disclosed. Is it only medical errors? Will you include near misses?

8. If there are some circumstances that are mandatory while others are discretionary. For example, your organization may want all medical errors to be disclosed, or you may consider disclosure on a case-by-case basis.

9. "How" to disclose. Consider whether you want to provide information to your healthcare providers on "how" to disclose, and if so, how much information you will provide to them regarding the mechanics of disclosure.

10. Addressing "when" to disclose. Consider whether including information on when disclosure needs to take place. Is it as soon as possible after the event?

You may struggle with some of these issues. Reach a consensus with your committee. Next, follow through with your organization's approval and implementation process. When you roll out your disclosure program to your organization, your policy will be in place and you can provide educational programming for your healthcare providers.

Action Steps:
- Have your disclosure committee develop your disclosure policy.
- Work through the analysis of what you want your policy to address and how.
- Adopt the policy and procedure through your organizational structure.
- Publish it to the organization.

Step 3: Roll Out the Program to the Entire Organization

Now let's obtain the commitment of the entire organization to successfully launch your disclosure program. This means education. Hold organization-wide seminars for your physicians and nurses. This is another good opportunity to get trainers or consultants involved in the process to assist you. **At a minimum,** providers (physicians, nurses, and technicians) should understand the disclosure concept and its benefits, know about the policy, and know who to call for advice and counsel on disclosure after an adverse event.

Critical to the success of this is that everyone understands how disclosure is a positive concept for *them* and patients. Medicine is a stressed profession with a lot of demands. If disclosure appears to be just more mandates — more work — then it will meet with resistance or worse. The reality is that when doctors and nurses understand disclosure, they will be fine with it ... back to education and its importance.

The educational program should stress the importance, the roots, and the value of disclosure. The message of the training for providers should be that disclosure is something you intuitively want to do, will put you in a better liability position, and is great for patients!

Other options exist for rolling out your disclosure program, and what you do is dependent on your organizational structure — number of facilities, providers, and staff. It may be a combination of live educational programming along with video educational programming, train the trainer, webcasts, and/or in-services. You may decide to hold live programs for all physicians and follow that by live educational programming for staff. Train-the-trainer programs can be incorporated and are useful for larger organizations.

Action Step: Provide educational programming to the healthcare team.

Step 4: Train the Disclosure Team

Your disclosure program should include establishing a disclosure team, or a group of individuals who receive additional, intense training on disclosure — how, when, what. You should carefully select your disclosure team, and they should be individuals committed to disclosure. At a hospital system, the team could include physician leaders, risk managers, a head nurse, a chaplain, and many others. At a doctor's practice, perhaps it is simply that everyone is a member of the disclosure team! The size of your disclosure team will depend on your program and organizational structure. Consider, for example: Will you have coverage 24-7 by at least one of these individuals? Do you need 24-7 coverage by more than one individual? Do you need a department head and an individual from every department? These are the types of issues that a disclosure consultant can help you to determine.

We often call disclosure team individuals "communication facilitators." Disclosure team members should become experts in disclosure and be ready to help providers deliver news to patients and to families. The hope is that individual providers will have to disclose on rare and infrequent occasions, so it should not be a surprise that providers will be "rusty" and forgetful of how to properly disclose to patients and families after adverse events. This is where a trained disclosure team helps. Disclosure team members should have hands-on training. Role playing and discussing scenarios are extremely important. Small group workshops can also be held.

You can even implement a train-the-trainer type program. (this will often depend on the size of your organization and can be somewhat fluid).

We have had disclosure teams be a small core but grow to be small teams within every department with additional backup if and when necessary. Do not get bogged down with size — get started with good communication and those champions mentioned earlier in this chapter.

Action Steps:
- Identify and select your communication facilitators.
- Provide hands-on training.

Step 5: Keep the Program Alive!

After all your hard work, you will need to focus on keeping the program alive! If principles are not kept at the forefront, they will be forgotten or become "stale." If disclosure does not occur, everyone will lose faith. It will become another initiative that everyone thought was a good idea and was excited about ... but lost steam. Do not let this happen! Consider the following suggestions:

- Start your disclosure program small and publicize your success stories internally! (Remember to do so in a way that protects the confidentiality of the physicians and providers involved and the patient.)
- Provide support to those involved in a disclosure event. Unexpected or adverse events also take a toll on the providers and those providing the disclosure. A post-event support system can help providers who have disclosed receive the help and healing they need so they can effectively return to serving patients and families. This is actually an underestimated concept. When outcomes are not realized, the doctor feels a rainbow of emotions — none of them good.
- Keep educating. Hold in-services on disclosure and annual educational programs. Gear the programs specifically to nursing staff, to physicians, to new employees, and to the disclosure team. Each will have different educational needs.
- Importantly, learn from the process. Disclosure is really a part of event management. Use the lessons learned to reduce the risk of future similar occurrences. This must be done in a blame-free manner. Review and discuss disclosed cases so that process improvements can take place. Learn from your mistakes and improve your healthcare delivery systems! Risk managers, patient safety officers, and business managers will value this aspect of your disclosure program.

- Educate the local trial bar about your disclosure program. The message is simple: Legitimate cases will be handled fairly and swiftly, but nonmeritorious claims will never be settled. Consider the following quote from Richard Boothman of the University of Michigan Health System:

> "I believe the word is out that if they (the trial bar) have a legitimate case, they share all the details with us, including their experts' reports and interviews with the family. I also believe that if they have a marginal or questionable case, they do not bother any more because they know we will fight those aggressively with the best of lawyers and best of experts."[22]

- Finally, please share your story. The more hospitals and insurers that tell Sorry Works! and disclosure success stories, the sooner disclosure and apology will be the norm. Share your story at conferences and with trade and popular media, always carefully protecting confidentiality but letting your peers know ... it works!

Remember, the end goal is development of a program — not a policy. Policies sit on the shelf and collect dust, whereas programs are literally living, breathing creatures. You need a plan, and this chapter provides you with the framework to accomplish a successful disclosure program.

Action Steps:
- Publish your success
- Continue with education
- Provide support

Review Points:

- Leadership commitment and buy-in
- A disclosure policy and procedure
- Roll out the program to the entire institution.
- Train the disclosure team.
- Keep the program alive!

Chapter 6

How to Apologize to Patients and Families

Remember, "I'm sorry" (or an expression of empathy) is different than an "apology" (or accepting responsibility). How you do either takes skill and training. This chapter provides you with the "how tos" of "I'm sorry" and "apology."

While the number of stories about Sorry Works! are promising and extremely compelling, a nagging question still persists for many healthcare professionals. How exactly do I say, "I'm sorry," without the patient getting the idea that I am admitting negligence? How exactly do I apologize to a patient or family? How do I accept responsibility in the right way? These are fair questions: Empathy and apology are not found on the course syllabi at most medical schools (although they should be). Physicians are not alone with this feeling. Although we are a forgiving nation, most Americans have trouble saying, "I'm sorry." All you have to do is pick up a newspaper or magazine to see politicians, athletes, movie stars, and others trying to apologize:

"For me to be at a comedy club and flip out and say this crap, I'm deeply, deeply sorry."[23] Michael Richards (you recognize him as Kramer from the TV show *Seinfeld*) apologized to the nation on the David Letterman show for racially charged language used during a comedy routine. This was part of his statement...and he hired a crisis expert before apologizing!

"It is with a great amount of shame that I stand before you and tell you I have betrayed your trust."[24] Marion Jones, Olympic gold medalist, apologized to the nation for lying about using steroids. *USA Today* did not buy it.[25]

Of course, bedrooms, kitchens, and coffee shops across America are the scenes of poorly delivered apologies day in and day out too:

"Honey, I don't understand why you are getting so emotional about this...I am sorry if I hurt your feelings. But, you know, you have some blame in all of this too! Can't you get over it so we can move on?"

Relationship experts can help couples apologize, but what is important in apologizing to your significant other is not necessarily important when a healthcare provider apologizes to a patient. We are here to help you empathize and apologize to your patients!

<u>*How to Say, "I'm sorry" — Expressing Empathy*</u>

You must always empathize, or say, *"I'm sorry."* This is true no matter what the circumstances, whether or not a medical error has occurred, and whether or not you are at fault. Your empathy must be heartfelt, and it must be a thread or theme through every discussion with the patient and/or family. This means if an adverse event occurred without error or liability attaching, say, *"I'm sorry."* This also means if an adverse event occurred where liability does attach (standard of care was breached and was the cause of injury or harm) then you must also say, *"I'm sorry."* In the second instance, you will also need to apologize (accept responsibility) (which is discussed later in this chapter). At the outset, how do you say, *"I'm sorry"*?

Immediately after an adverse event occurs, your disclosure team may be alerted and can help with the initial step of empathy. The provider should always express empathy, and remember that context is essential. Perhaps your conversation would go like this:

"I am sorry this happened. I want you to know that we are conducting an investigation to learn what happened, and as we learn information you will learn information. OK?

Here is my business card if you have any questions or need assistance. The number on the card rings to a live person 24 hours a day/7 days a week. Also, as relatives come to the hospital please have them call the number on the card if they have any questions or concerns...myself or someone from my staff will be happy to speak with them.

The nurses and physicians attending to the care of your son understand his current condition, and they are committed to working with you and your family.

Is there anything else we can do for you or your family at this point? We have counseling services available that may help you including pastoral services. Would you be interested in speaking with anyone from social services or a counselor?

Do you have any questions? If not now, but questions later arise after I leave, please call the number on the card, and I would be happy to answer your questions."

Notice that we said, "Sorry," but no blame was accepted or assigned. The first step of the disclosure process is not a true apology...it is simply empathy and compassion. It is also good customer service. In reading the dialogue above you can see that the speaker literally trying to pull the family closer to the institution, just like a good customer service program will literally make the injured/aggrieved customer their best friend in the immediate aftermath. Also, you can see that we said only what we know. We do not infer or make guesses…we simply stay in the proper zone of being empathetic and promising an investigation to learn the facts.

This initial disclosure is all about rebuilding trust with customers. Patients and families place an enormous amount of trust in healthcare professionals. Indeed, there is no other service relationship in our society where one party places so much trust (and faith) in another party. When an adverse event occurs (whether there was an error or not), the trust is put to an extreme test. In many cases, trust is broken and has to be earned back. Following an adverse event, a healthcare institution and their insurer should do everything to bring the patient and family closer and embrace them. That is good customer service, and the first 24 hours after an event are the most critical. It is what any good customer-centered company does for their customers after mishaps — think Disney, The Ritz-Carlton, or Southwest Airlines. What do these companies do after something goes wrong? Answer: They make the customer their best friend.

Below are some more examples of expressing empathy:

- *"I'm very sorry about your loss. I was saddened to hear of it and offer you my condolences and the condolences of my staff. We all enjoyed your son and caring for him. We will miss him."*
- *"I'm sorry you feel this way. I want to talk about what happened and help you understand it and what we are going to do next so that you can be assured that we are doing everything we can to care for you and support you."*

Some phrases to stay away from:

- *"These things happen all the time. It just happened to a patient of mine yesterday."*
- *"You are going to just have to tough it out."*
- *"You're overreacting."*

- *"You should have known that the pill was not the right one. You should have told the nurse."*
- *"If I had seen the lab report results, I would have ordered a CT scan, but I did not. It's all my PA's fault for not letting me know."*
- *"It's all the radiologist's fault."*
- *"I wish I hadn't ignored the symptoms of abdominal pain. I just thought they were not significant."*
- *"It's not my fault. You should have..."*
- *"I'm never going to work with that doctor again. The next time I need a cardiology consult, I will refuse to work with him."*
- *"I should have listened to the rumors. I heard that consultant had three patients die last month."*
- *"I did everything I could. I did hear that Dr. Jones was fired from the last practice he worked with. It looks like there was good reason for that!"*

You need to stay away from blaming others or jumping to conclusions before all of the facts are in. Stick simply with empathy at the outset. Then investigate and determine whether more is needed.

With the empathy placed and information shared with the patient/family, you are ready to investigate the circumstances and determine whether an apology is warranted. Apologizing may seem like an easy task, but when it is you that is at fault, when it is your reputation on the line, when it is your insurance that is affected, when it is your privileges at risk, it is a very difficult task emotionally.

Please note: An apology, which includes admission of fault, only happens after an investigation reveals that the standard of care has been breached and it is causally related to the injury. Do not make an apology until you are ready! You cannot take it back!

How to Apologize and Accept Fault

Any effective, meaningful apology has four basic elements:[26]

(1) Empathy or "sorry"
(2) Admission of fault (*"I made a mistake — It's my fault"*)
(3) Explanation of what happened and how it will be prevented from happening again
(4) An offer of compensation or some sort of fix to the problem that has been created

> **Effective, meaningful apologies have four basic elements:**
>
> 1) Empathy or *"sorry"*
>
> 2) Admission of fault (*"I made a mistake — It's my fault"*)
>
> 3) Explanation of what happened and how it will be prevented from happening again
>
> 4) Offer of compensation or some sort of fix to the problem that was created

The four elements must be present for an apology to be perceived as real and meaningful by the patient/family. Apologies that include these four elements will reduce and — in many cases — eliminate anger felt by the aggrieved party. Relationships and trust will be restored. However, if any of the four elements are missing, the aggrieved party will see the apology as hollow or meaningless and their anger will increase, along with the risk of litigation and other forms of retribution.

It is important to explain what happened and how it will be prevented from happening again. This should all have been part of your investigation process. True change cannot occur without knowing exactly what happened. Patients want to know what happened. They also want to know how it will be prevented again. If you tell patients how it will be prevented from happening again, you must ensure that those steps are taken. It may be a new process, incorporation of a new tool, a new hire, education, or even firing.

When it comes to compensation or a fix, we are really talking about resolution. How can you bring closure to this situation? Words alone may not be enough. Patients will have real problems as a result of the error that need to be fixed — by you, your organization, and/or your insurer.

"The apology is one thing, but my husband will be laid up for six months because of their error. Who is going to pay the bills and put food on the table? I guess I will have to sue these doctors!"

Sometimes it will simply be monetary compensation, but think outside the box. Listen to their issues and think of creative ways to resolve them:

- Lodging, meals for loved ones
- Continuing medical education for the healthcare provider
- An endowment in a loved one's name
- A scholarship in a loved one's name
- Paying off a house mortgage
- Remodeling a home for wheelchair access
- A structured settlement for children of the patient
- Childcare expenses
- Lost wages for the period of recovery
- Naming a lecture series on errors in honor of their loved one
- Involving the patient/family in quality improvement processes at the hospital

Recognize that for payments made (no matter what the form of payment) in response to a medical error or any negligent basis, you will need to have the patient sign a release, releasing you from any claims of liability related to the matter at hand. Legal counsel should be involved to ensure that the release is valid and will hold up in court should it be challenged. The release will provide protections from any future claims made by the patient and/or family based on the underlying negligence. It's not a lottery. The patient should not be able to reach an agreement with you and then later decide that he wants more money and sue.

Word of caution: As has been mentioned, an apology involving the four elements should only be delivered to a patient or family after an investigation has *proven* an error or breach of standard of care occurred, as well as a causative connection. It is hard, if not impossible, to "un-ring" the apology bell. Make sure you have all the facts in place before apologizing. Remember, "I'm sorry" just by itself can be and is very meaningful. It makes every situation a little better, assuming it is part of an overall enhanced communication strategy. The four steps of apology are reserved for those cases as explained above where due diligence has been completed.

> **"Make sure you have all the facts in place before apologizing."**

"OK, great, I understand the four elements of apology and when I should apologize, but how do I actually deliver an apology should an investigation show that an error was committed?"

It starts with the right attitude, which includes the understanding that disclosure and apology is not about the doctors, nurses, hospital, or the insurance company — it is about the patients and family: The customer. You must think how your words and nonverbal communication and other actions will be received by your customers.

Take a different perspective by placing yourself in __that__ position.

Your customers are going to be closely scrutinizing you and your colleagues throughout the disclosure and apology process. Their emotions are raw. They are literally mourning the injury or death caused by the medical error. The trust they placed in you, your colleagues, and the institution has been violated. The relationship has been damaged. They desperately want to rebuild their trust in you, but any slip up (even unintended) will send them tumbling back down the hill. Be careful. Think this through.

We have already discussed how to effectively empathize, and you will need to continue to empathize in your apology discussion.

Remember, you have in place an event management infrastructure to support your apology and disclosure. Use it and use the information below as your checklist. First, let's set the stage.

- Select a neutral meeting to apologize and to disclose.

    Schedule a disclosure meeting at a time and place convenient and comfortable for the patient/family. It may well be at the hospital. However, it could also be at a later point in time. Remember, disclosure is all about the customer. Make it convenient for them, but also make it private and comfortable.

- Clear your calendar — do not put a time limit on the meeting.

    Clear off your morning or afternoon calendar. Do not assume the disclosure meeting will last an hour and schedule a patient or another meeting immediately afterwards. You may either rush through the disclosure meeting (which is bad) or you may be forced to cancel on the other patient, which is poor service for that individual. More importantly, you will not feel comfortable in the disclosure meeting and the customers will pick up on your negative verbal and nonverbal cues. You do not want to rush through the disclosure meeting — take all time you need and the family needs. Furthermore, after the meeting, you and your colleagues will want time to decompress and review. Take all the time necessary!

- Provide food, drinks, mints, tissues, and other necessary items.

- Provide comfortable chairs, good temperature, and a clean meeting room.

    This almost seems like common sense, but many a meeting has been destroyed by uncomfortable chairs, a room that was too hot or cold, or a table that was covered by crumbs, half-eaten cookies, and spilled drinks from the previous meeting. Make the sure the room is ready for the disclosure meeting.

- Special needs? Know your customers!

   Scout out the patient and family ahead of time. Know them. Understand them. How many members of the family plan to attend the meeting? Is the room big enough to accommodate everyone? Are there enough chairs? Is the table big enough? Does anyone have a wheelchair or other special needs? Know your customers!

- Details, details, details

   It sounds morbid, but think like a funeral home director. Walk into a high-quality funeral home and every detail is covered so the family can focus on their one job: Mourning. Dealing with an adverse medical event involves mourning too, especially if there is a death or major injury. So, when planning the meeting make sure every detail is covered so the customers can focus on the apology and disclosure and begin the process of healing and moving on with their lives.

OK, so the stage is set for a successful apology and disclosure meeting. So how exactly do you apologize? Again, below is an important checklist.

- Have a plan.

   Have a plan in place: What will be discussed, who will be present, who will take the lead, what is the desired result, and how are you going to get there? This should be coordinated through your event management program.

- Practice.

   Practice what you are going to say and how you are going to say it before the meeting/discussion. Use a mirror so that you can see how you may be perceived by others. You can even work with legal counsel to practice through videotaping. If you do practice with video, be sure to do so with legal counsel involved so you can protect those practice sessions under attorney-client privilege. You do not want a plaintiff's lawyer using your practice sessions, your goof-ups, in front of a jury!

- As you start the meeting, remember to turn off cell phones and pagers.

  "Mrs. Jones, I want to tell you how sorry we are about the mistake that injured your BEEP! BEEP! BEEP! BEEP! BEEP! Now, where was I? Oh, yes, your husband and how we injured him. We are so...BEEP, BEEP, BEEP, BEEP..."

  Get the idea? Just like the movie theater, put your pagers and cell phones on mute at the start of the meeting. Do *not* set your pager to vibrate, because your customers will hear that too and wonder why you are not answering it. A better idea is to leave your pager and/or cell phone with a responsible person who can monitor it for you during the meeting, and if there is a real emergency that person can slip you a note or whisper in your ear and you can politely excuse yourself from the meeting.

- Sit down with the patient and family. Do not stand or lecture.

  Physicians are used to being authority figures. Sit down at the same table with the customers and look them in the eye. Act respectful and courteous. If you feel the urge to lecture or stand up, do not do it. In this meeting, you are *not* the chief of staff or head of anesthesia with an advanced degree. You want to relate: One human being apologizing to other human beings and asking for forgiveness. Be humble, be contrite, and show it. Get on the same side of the table!

- Talk slowly, and do not dominate the conversation. Allow the patient and family to interject and ask questions.

  Healthcare professionals have a tendency to dominate a conversation. Not here, not in this meeting. Talk slowly and deliberately as you work through the apology. Use common language. Do not use too much scientific or medical jargon. Use common language: It was a heart attack that was missed, not a myocardial infarction. Also, allow and even encourage the customers to interrupt with questions and statements. Remember, this meeting is all about the customer, although we often find it helpful and therapeutic to the doctor.

- Silence is OK!

    Silence and "pregnant pauses" in meetings can feel painful, especially when you are a busy person who is used to being in charge and talking really fast. But silence is OK and even necessary in disclosure meetings. Silence gives your customers time to absorb what you are saying and formulate questions or responses...the questions and responses you will need to hear to ensure you are connecting. Silence is OK...silence is respectful.

- In effect, ask your customers to repeat back what you said by asking them questions.

    You want to make sure your patients and families are correctly receiving the information you are trying to convene. Remember, your customers are likely in an emotionally traumatized state, so you need to make an extra effort to make sure you are connecting by occasionally asking them to repeat back what you said or ask them some simple questions. If they are not receiving the information, you will need to review the information, or you may even need to schedule another meeting when they are emotionally ready to listen better. Use your judgment.

- The "s" word: "Sorry". Say it!

    Say you are sorry. Do not say you *"regret the mistake,"* *"feel bad,"* or *"wish the episode hadn't happened,"* but say, *"I'm sorry."* Patients and families want to hear you say the "s" word. It is literally the gold standard and has special value to injured patients and families. They want to hear the word from you. Look your customers in the eye and say, *"I'm sorry."*

- When appropriate, as discussed earlier, admit fault.

    Take ownership of the mistake.

    "I made a mistake"... "It was my fault"... "I accept full responsibility for this unfortunate situation"... "We committed an error"...etc, etc.

    "Sorry" is one word, but admission of fault shows people you have real character and are truly owning up to the problem. Admission of fault is necessary for patients and families to forgive you. Sorry without admission of fault will ring hollow and heighten anger and suspicion with your customers in the circumstances where an apology is needed.

- Explain — slowly — how the error happened, to the extent you know, and how it will be prevented in the future.

  Tell customers how the error happened and how you, your colleagues, and the institution have learned from the mistake(s) and what you will do to make sure the same mistake(s) are not repeated. Patients and families desperately want to hear this information from healthcare providers. Customers want to know that their suffering was not in vain and medicine will improve. This is a very important to patients and families, especially when they expect and desire to receive treatment in the same hospital again.

- Answer all questions truthfully and honesty. It is OK to say you do not know the answer to a question.

  The explanation of events that caused the error(s) will undoubtedly lead to questions from the customers. Take these questions seriously and behave in a correct manner if you do not know the answer to a particular question.

  Medical school teaches physicians to always be on their toes and be ready for difficult questions thrown by an instructor or senior physician. The fact is that life is an open-book exam. Nobody knows all the answers to all the questions, and customers understand this truism. It is OK to say I do not know.

  "I don't know the answer to your question, Mrs. Jones, but I can assure you we will continue to research this, and I will be back in touch with you in the next day or so. Is this OK?"

  Very acceptable. But if you try to fake your way through a question, most customers will detect your half-baked answers and resent you, and once you are caught in a lie the disclosure process is ruined. Get ready for a lawsuit.

- Allow customers to vent and rant — do not take it personally.

  Patients and families will receive a wealth of emotionally charged information in a disclosure meeting. Their initial response may be anger, shock, and rage, and they may express these feelings with shouting, cursing, crying, and accusations. Do not take any of it personally. Let your customers vent. Do not engage in a shouting match, become defensive, or get sucked into an argument. Simply respond by saying, *"I can only imagine how this feels for you, and being angry at me, my colleagues, and this institution is completely understandable. I am so sorry about all of this. I am truly sorry."*

  Let them continue to vent and allow the anger to drain out of them. Look for the appropriate opening to continue the discussion. If no opening presents itself, the disclosure process may need to continue with a second meeting on another day. Provide space and time for cooler heads to prevail.

- Communicate.

  Communication is not just what you say, but it is also how you say it. Be mindful of your word choice, the tone of your voice, and your demeanor. Patients recognize insincerity. Be sincere. Do not look at your watch (it only suggests that you are in a hurry). Even if the discussion is over the phone, patients, while they cannot see you, they can get a sense of the tone of your voice and determine whether you are being sincere. Do not become angry or judgmental.

- Listen.

  Truly listen to what the patient/family have to say. This means not only what they say but also how they say it. Patients will know when you are not listening and are not taking them seriously.

- Express gratitude.

  Express gratitude for bringing a situation to your attention, if that is the case.

- When anger has dissipated, begin discussing compensation.

    When the time is right, begin discussing compensation. Express to the customer and their legal counsel, if present, that you want to fairly and quickly compensate for the injury you and your institution have caused. Ask questions about wages/salaries, home and family expenses, and expenses from the injury/death so you can begin to formulate the amount of compensation needed.

- Compensation discussions may take several meetings.

    Compensation may be discussed and negotiated over several meetings. The first meeting may involve simply asking questions and getting a better understanding of the customers' financial situation and needs. Between the first and second meetings you and your disclosure team may develop a compensation proposal. Be sure to involve people on your team from risk management and legal counsel who understand the value of injuries and wrongful deaths.

    It is a process. You will try to meet their needs by making an offer. Undoubtedly, your customers and their counsel will counteroffer with a number that is on the higher end of the scale. Listen to what your customers and their legal counsel say constitutes fair compensation. Even though their number is higher than your original offer, it does not mean they are necessarily trying to be unfair or fleece you. Ask questions and listen. Because anger has dissipated (or even eliminated), you can have a discussion about what is fair and reasonable compensation. Take advantage of the situation and talk with your customers and their attorney! It is a process. Try to keep the discussion on an objective level. Risk managers are experienced and often very good at this, as are representatives of your insurer.

- Be fair but firm — you're not an open checkbook!

    You want to be fair with your customers and their legal counsel, but you must be firm. All unreasonable and outrageous requests will be denied, and if they persist let them know you are not afraid to have the courts make the ultimate decision. That decision will be basically limited to determining the value of damages.

- Disclosure may be an extended affair — stay in touch with the patient and their family.

  Medical errors can be long-term affairs. One or two disclosure meetings *may* not completely resolve the situation. You may need to continually reach out and communicate with patients and their family members for an extended period of time to make sure they understand all the issues and are comfortable with the resolution. Remember, disclosure and apology are ultimately about rebuilding trust and relationships, so be a friend and stay in touch with people! Do not ever let patients and families feel abandoned or they may pay you back with litigation or other acts of retribution.

- Summarize the discussion and next steps.

  At the end of the meeting, summarize for the patient/family what was discussed, what their concerns were, how they will be addressed, and what the next steps are.

- Document.

  Consistent with the discussion on event management, document the meeting/discussion.

This extensive checklist of items list should not overwhelm you and your colleagues. Yes, disclosure and apology can be a lot to think about, especially if you have not been trained or experienced in these matters. Prior to a disclosure meeting, the participants should engage in role plays to "practice" what they are going to say and how they will react to customer feedback. However, you do not want to develop a script…disclosure and apology must come from the heart. Customers will detect scripted apologies and may feel like they are being snowed over. Practice, yes; but scripting, no.

Examples of effective apologies:

- *"I'm sorry that you are experiencing side effects from the medication dosage. I accidentally wrote 30 milligrams instead of 3.0 milligrams on your prescription. I have taken steps in my practice to ensure that this does not happen again. We have implemented JCAHO recommendations for number nomenclature on prescriptions that should reduce future risk of* similar incidents. *The important thing for you to know with your care is that the side effects are temporary and they will not be associated with any permanent damage. I will be happy to reimburse you for the cost of a second prescription and your salary for the two days that you were off work."*

- *"I'm sorry that I misread your x-ray. I have no excuse, and can only hope that you understand that medicine is not a perfect science. I do my best to read every x-ray with the utmost of care and diligence. Sometimes, a miss occurs. We have looked at ways to reduce the number of misreads that occur as a result of your circumstances. We have instituted a new policy that ensures quality assurance reviews every morning of the previous day's reads. We know that this has worked well in other practices. What I would like to do for you is pay for your surgery that is now needed to repair the fracture and provide you with compensation that will reimburse your medical expenses associated with this fracture and any pain you have been experiencing. I have received an estimate from your surgeon on the costs of your surgery and related medical expenses, as well as an estimate for medications and rehab that will be needed. Given this, I want to provide you with $15,000."*

- *"I'm sorry that I did not see the results of your mammogram. If I had, I would have referred you to an oncologist at that time. We have reviewed the circumstances, and I have discovered that for some unknown reason, your lab report ended up in the medical chart without being initialed by anyone. We have in place a requirement at our practice that all lab reports are initialed when they are reviewed. It appears that did not happen here. In efforts to reduce the risk of this happening again, I have hired a nurse whose sole job is to review all incoming laboratory reports and x-rays. When she sees a report with an abnormal result, she is required to notify the patient's physician so that appropriate next steps can be taken, including notification to the patient. The good news is that we have not lost much time, I have called in a favor and have gotten you an appointment for tomorrow with an oncologist. The oncologist will discuss with you your treatment options. I would like to stay involved with your care, and your oncologist will keep me informed. Please feel free to reach out to me throughout this process if you have any questions. Again, I am truly sorry for what has happened, but I do feel that we have your care on track now, and that you will have a good result."*

Examples of ineffective apologies:

- *"As the doctor here I can tell you this situation is just horrible for me. I feel terrible. I wish this hadn't happened. You know, I shouldn't be telling you this, but Nurse Betty shouldn't have given those drugs to your daughter... that's the reason she's on life support. OK? Oh, there's my beeper, I need to run. Bye."*

- *"I was on call when the leak was discovered. Dr. Jones should have paged me, but he did not. I know he told you he did, but he's wrong. It's all his fault."*

- *"I'm sorry you think something went wrong, but a cut of the common bile duct is a known complication of this procedure. I know I did not discuss it with you prior to surgery, but everyone knows it is a risk."*

- *"I'm sorry that I performed surgery on your right leg instead of your left, but it is all the nurse's fault. She placed an "x" on the left leg, and I thought it meant not to touch that leg. She should have put a "yes" on your left leg. Everyone knows that, and that is what our hospital policy says to do."*

It all boils down to three steps:
(1) Empathy
(2) Investigation
(3) Apology and disclosure

What if your investigation reveals that no error occurred?

You provided initial empathy to the patient/family and have told them you would investigate the matter. Above, we explained how to apologize when the investigation reveals that an error occurred, but what if none occurred? You must still contact the patient or family and schedule a meeting with them. In this meeting, continue with your empathy (*"We are sorry this happened"*) and explain the findings of the investigation. You may also want to share the records of the investigation with the patient/family. For example, if the autopsy report determines that the cause of death was natural, show the family the autopsy report and explain it to them. Answer any questions they may have. In this meeting, you need to show what you did with your investigation, why it was appropriate, and the results. No settlement is offered.

What if the patient/family still think otherwise? You have some options, and which you choose will be dependent on the circumstances. You can simply wait to see if a lawyer takes on the case. Plaintiff lawyers in advance of filing suit should request the patient's medical records. When this occurs, it should be a telltale sign that a plaintiff's lawyer is investigating the patient's care, and, at this point, you can have your legal counsel reach out to the plaintiff's counsel in an attempt to dissuade him from filing a lawsuit.

Your lawyer may offer to have the plaintiff's lawyer talk with the expert that reviewed your care and determined that your care was appropriate. Your lawyer may offer to meet with the patient and the lawyer, along with you.

However, before a patient ever reaches a lawyer, you may decide that the patient would be best served to talk with your expert. This should not be done without legal counsel involvement, but it can be powerful.

Ultimately, if all of your care was appropriate, your case should be defended to the end. It is the only way the right message can be sent to patients and attorneys: We will not settle cases where our care met the standard of care.

Finally, this chapter demonstrates why it is important to have a disclosure *program* that is administered by a team of professionals in your organization from administration, risk management, legal, and the medical staff. This team needs to be trained on all the details of disclosure and through the program be prepared to offer support and help to your medical professionals, who will be disclosing and apologizing on rare and infrequent occasions.

Review Points:

- Say you are sorry after an event without admitting fault.
- Include the four steps of apology when you need to apologize.
- If an investigation reveals no causative error, continue to empathize but do not admit fault.
- Practice!

CHAPTER 7

DO YOU NEED A LAW TO APOLOGIZE?

"I would never introduce a doctor's apology in court. It is my job to make a doctor look bad in front of a jury, and telling the jury the doctor apologized and tried to do the right thing kills my case." — President, South Carolina Trial Lawyers Association, testimony before South Carolina Senate, September 2005

This quote stands in stark contrast to conventional wisdom, but it is right on the money. Unfortunately, healthcare and insurance professionals have been errantly informed for years not to apologize lest it be used against them in court. *"Say you're sorry and you're dead in court,"* is the mantra. Not so, as mentioned previously, as long as apology and disclosure are done right and understanding the vast difference between a sincere showing of empathy and an apology accepting responsibility. Both done in the right way under the right circumstances have powerful positive legal consequences.

Further, across the country, state legislatures have enacted laws that provide some form of immunity to physicians and other healthcare providers for apologies if a lawsuit is initiated. The impact of these laws includes providing the environment in which healthcare providers feel comfortable with apologizing to patients and families with less fear of repercussions. However, these disclosure laws, though they have good public relations value (physicians feel better about disclosing and apologizing), often have little legal utility. Disclosure builds a great defense if a lawsuit is still initiated, and enlightened defense counsel shouldn't want to omit the disclosure process from the evidence. In conclusion, though apology laws are helpful, they are not needed or necessary for a hospital or insurer to implement a disclosure program, and defense counsel should rarely employ such laws in defending a physician or hospital.

Disclosure: Medical Ethics and the Law

The reasons to disclose for the patient and family have been discussed and have their grounding in law, ethics, and common sense. Patients have a right to know. Ethical standards have been promulgated by the American Medical Association, the Joint Commission on Accreditation of Healthcare Organizations (JCAHO), and the American College of Physicians Ethics Manual.

The American Medial Association *Code of Medical Ethics* provides:

> It is a fundamental ethical requirement that a physician should at all times deal honestly and openly with patients. Patients have a right to know their past and present medical status and to be free of any mistaken beliefs concerning their conditions. Situations occasionally occur in which a patient suffers significant medical complications that may have resulted from the physician's mistake or judgment. In these situations, the physician is ethically required to inform the patient of all the facts necessary to ensure understanding of what has occurred. Only through full disclosure is a patient able to make informed decisions regarding future medical care.
>
> Ethical responsibility includes informing patients of changes in their diagnoses resulting from retrospective review of test results or any other information. This obligation holds even though the patient's medical treatment or therapeutic options may not be altered by the new information.
>
> Concern regarding legal liability which might result following truthful disclosure should not affect the physician's honesty with a patient.[27]

In summary, the Code of Medical Ethics requires disclosure from an ethical viewpoint and further states that concerns over legal liability that may result from that disclosure are no reason to be untruthful. JCAHO's accreditation standards address the ethical considerations, providing: "Patients and, when appropriate, their families are informed about the outcomes of care, including unanticipated outcomes."[28] The value of JCAHO's position is that it means that the movement for healthcare provider disclosure extends to the hospitals, and accordingly, the approach with disclosure can be collaborative between the healthcare professional and the hospital.

However, healthcare providers as noted above have traditionally been fearful to apologize to patients and families, believing that the apology will be construed as an admission of fault or guilt. This fear is not without support as plaintiff attorneys have used healthcare provider words against them in the courtroom; however, it is time to change this view and to have disclosure and showing of empathy used for healthcare providers instead of against them, and the apology laws help to fuel the environment needed to effectuate change.

In 1986, Massachusetts was the first state to enact a sympathy/apology law, and it provided:

> "Statements, writings or benevolent gestures expressing sympathy or a general sense of benevolence relating to the pain, suffering or death of a person involved in an accident and made to such person or to the family of such person shall be inadmissible as evidence of an admission of liability in a civil action."[29]

It was not until 1998 that the next sympathy/apology law was enacted. In total, since the Massachusetts law was enacted, 33 more states have enacted some form of a sympathy/apology law, providing immunity protections to healthcare providers (at the time this book was written). (See Appendix A for a complete list of those states and the relevant statutes.) The most laws were enacted in 2005, with 13 states enacting laws with immunity provisions. The components of the sympathy/apology laws vary, and they generally include:

- Protections in certain actions (i.e., civil actions, wrongful death actions only, arbitrations, administrative proceedings);
- What is protected (i.e., written statements, oral statements, and/or conduct);
- What content is protected (i.e., affirmations, gestures, expressions of apology or sympathy, expressions of fault, "sorry," offers to undertake corrective action);
- Who is protected (healthcare providers and/or employees of the healthcare provider);

- Who is the statement or conduct directed to (patient, relative of the patient, patient's survivors, healthcare decision maker for the patient, friend of the patient or family);
- What does the apology or sympathy relate to (i.e., an accident, an unanticipated outcome, an event, patient injury or pain);
- What protection is afforded (i.e., inadmissible as evidence of admission of liability, inadmissible as admission against interest, protected from examination in a deposition)

Most states do *not* protect statements or admissions of fault. Among those, the terminology varies:

- Statement of fault
- Admission of liability or fault
- Fault
- Statement of fault, negligence, or culpable conduct

The end result is essentially the same and attempts to promote an environment where healthcare professionals feel that their discussions of disclosure and empathy with patients and family will not later be used against them.

Colorado, on the other hand, enacted one of the broader state laws, which includes protections for a healthcare provider's actions and conduct and specifically protects words or acts that express fault. The law was intended to be broad in efforts to promote an open relationship between physicians and their patients.[30] Georgia, South Carolina, Connecticut, and Arizona also recently shielded words such as "mistake" and "error."

Some state laws incorporate a timing element. For example, in Vermont, the statement or conduct must be made within 30 days of when the provider knew or should have known of the consequences of the error, in order to be protected. This approach may take away from some of the goals of the sympathy/apology laws.

The authors believe that a combination of various components of these statutes and more makes for the most effective sympathy/apology law. (A draft model law is contained in Appendix B.)

Beyond the sympathy/apology laws, some states have gone a step further and have enacted mandatory disclosure requirements. To date, eight (8) states have enacted such laws: California, Florida, Nevada, New Jersey, Oregon, Pennsylvania, Vermont, and Washington.[31] Pennsylvania was the first state to require a statutory duty to notify patients in writing of a "serious event." It provides:

> A medical facility through an appropriate designee shall provide written notification to a patient affected by a serious event or, with the consent of the patient, to an available family member or designee within seven days of the occurrence or discovery of a serious event. If the patient is unable to give consent, the notification shall be given to an adult member of the immediate family. If an adult member of the immediate family cannot be identified or located, notification shall be given to the closest adult family member. For unemancipated patients who are under 18 years of age, the parent or guardian shall be notified in accordance with this subsection...Notification under this subsection shall not constitute an acknowledgment or admission of liability.[32]

The concept of these mandatory disclosure laws is premised on the ethical foundation, which can benefit patients and healthcare providers, when the law is satisfied in an appropriate fashion. However, admittedly and clearly, they are not without drawbacks. Often patients view these letters as an indication that something "wrong" happened. In fact, the letters, unfortunately, are often written that way (perhaps, according to statute, almost necessarily so!). In these states it becomes critical to have a disclosure program in place so that the mandatory letter becomes part of the process and not the process itself. In this respect, the patient will receive their letter *after* communication has occurred and will read the letter in context. They will have already been told about the letter and the purpose of the letter, and the potential of the notice letter being taken out of context are greatly reduced.

The Pennsylvania law, for example, places the onus on the hospital facility to provide written notification to the patient/family within seven (7) days of the occurrence or discovery of a serious event. It is essential that even though it is the hospital's duty to comply with this law, the physicians be involved in the disclosure. In fact, hospitals should coordinate this process with their doctors. Remember, the letter *is* evidence. Healthcare providers and hospitals should use the letter to their advantage instead of disadvantage. There is a tendency to say as little as possible in the letter for fear of the letter being used against the hospital or healthcare provider. However, an alternative approach could be a well-balanced letter that informs the patient at the same time that it documents positive evidence.

At the federal level, Senators Hillary Rodham Clinton (D-NY) and Barack Obama (D-IL) introduced the Medical Error Disclosure and Compensation Act in 2005. It set forth a two-part approach, requiring expression of sympathy to be provided immediately to a patient and permitting other discussion of accountability to be made only after a full investigation was completed. The bill died in committee. The authors suggest that it is time to revisit federal legislation in this arena.

What if Your State Does Not Have a Law?

Sympathy/apology laws encourage physicians and healthcare professionals to overcome their cultural inhibitions about apology by providing the immunity protections that have seemingly held healthcare providers back. *"Hey, it's OK to apologize now...we won't get sued!"* However, the truth of the matter is that it has always been OK to say "sorry." In fact, as mentioned earlier, good communication after an adverse event is an important legal strategy to reduce the potential of the so-called "plus" in the courtroom.

After an adverse event, everything that occurs, but particularly what occurs in the first 24 hours, will often help determine whether or not the patient or family go to see a lawyer. It has been well established that two significant reasons they do so are out of anger or to obtain what they perceive as needed information: *"What really happened?"* When patients do not receive prompt information post-adverse event, they are forced to speculate what is almost always on the negative view. They become suspicious. Worse yet, they can hear different explanations that are not well coordinated and make it appear as if different versions are being offered. Perhaps their questions go unanswered, or worse, phone calls or requests for a meeting go unanswered. These actions (or inactions) drive them to a lawyer. This is also the type of behavior that plaintiff lawyers find attractive. It is the "plus" — behavior that when showcased in the courtroom in front of patients (jurors) can anger the jury and result in large awards at times more reflective of their reaction to the behavior than the actual damages! Jury consultants have confirmed and we have seen firsthand.

We must begin to realize that not only is disclosure and enhanced compassionate communication post-adverse event best for the patient and family, it is your best legal strategy and the reason apology-immunity laws have little legal value. As the quote at the beginning of this chapter says, trial lawyers like to demonize physician and hospital defendants. A claim of "cover-up" or the fact a family has to go to a lawyer to find out what happened certainly paves the way.

"All that my client wanted to know was what happened. Their son was in the ICU instead of home after what was described as a minor procedure. No one was saying anything. When they asked the nurse, she quickly turned away. One nurse actually asked if my client had talked to Dr. Smith. Well, they tried, but he never returned the call. They lost their son and have to sue to find out what really happened! Can you ladies and gentlemen imagine not knowing? Well, we will all find out this week..."

If apology and disclosure are done right, healthcare professionals and their institutions will reduce and importantly keep patients and families on the *same side of the table in the quest to find out what happened and what we need to do about it.* Patients should not feel as if they need help from a lawyer to do so.

There are cases where fault is not at question — but the parties cannot agree on the value of damages. Value is intensely subjective. Damages include both economic and noneconomic damages. The economic damages are often definable, but the noneconomic damages are far harder to value. For example, noneconomic damages include pain and suffering or loss of consortium (essentially loss of companionship). Sometimes this inability to easily determine the value of noneconomic damages can lead to nonresolution (because it is too hard!) and a lawsuit being filed. Most cases, in the hands of experienced lawyers, can resolve these difficult cases. At times mediation can help or even arbitrating among defendants who cannot agree on apportionment.

However, if the case proceeds to court, the provider and/or hospital will instruct defense counsel to argue the case only on the damages; fault will **not** be contested. Assuming the provider(s) made a reasonable monetary offer during the disclosure process, the plaintiff attorney will have scant evidence with which to inflame the jury. Always remember, it's hard — if not impossible — for a plaintiff's attorney to prosecute an honest, contrite defendant who made a good faith effort to fix a problem.

"But can an apology ever lead to a successful lawsuit?"

If an apology is hurried or botched, a lawsuit may be in the offing. What's a hurried apology? Admitting fault or assigning blame before an investigation is complete. Consider the following quotes that could be dangerous in the immediate aftermath of an adverse event:

"Sorry, we screwed up."

"I'm sorry I did this to you."

"Sorry. If I had read the lab reports differently, this would not have happened."

You must be careful, because you may be forced to eat those words if your investigation shows no error was committed, and then the family and their legal counsel may suspect a cover-up. Remember, it's hard to "un-ring" the apology bell.

"Well, of course they're now saying they didn't make mistake. But as your attorney, I can tell you the most honest moment in this whole chain of events is when that doctor came out of the operating room and spontaneously admitted to you that he made an error that led to your husband's death. There is a cover-up going on here and we will file a lawsuit to unearth the truth."

There are ways to show empathy without making a statement that will be used against you. For instance:

"During your husband's surgery a complication occurred. We are sorry this happened. We are going to do a complete evaluation to find out what exactly happened. We want to share that with you and answer any questions you have then and now. As far as the complication, remember when we discussed surgery in my office. Yes, that's right. I did draw pictures and gave your husband a copy of the form."

Remember, an apology — which includes admission of fault — is only offered after an investigation has proven an error occurred. Yes, always be in a hurry to empathize, but don't always be in a hurry to apologize.

What's a botched apology? An apology that is not heartfelt or sincere. An apology that deflects blame. Consider the following the examples:

"You know your husband shouldn't have had a high fat diet for all those years. He was in horrible shape and we did the best we could. Sorry."

"I know you feel bad about the loss of your wife, but I feel absolutely horrible. You have no idea what this is going to do my career!"

"I shouldn't be telling you this, but Nurse Jones has made several errors, and I think she gave your son the wrong drugs."

"Well, medicine is not only a science, but it's an art form too. This was a medical misadventure and these things do happen from time to time. No one is really at fault; it just happened and we regret it."

All of this was discussed in greater detail in chapter 6. The important point is that if apology and disclosure are done in a well-thought-through process, the result can be beneficial for the healthcare provider and the patient, and even reduce frequency and severity. You need not have a sympathy/apology law in your state to allow you to feel comfortable to do so; however, if your state does have one, it can only help to make you feel more comfortable. It in no way means you should approach the disclosure process any less carefully.

Review Points:

- The disclosure movement has taken hold, with 34 states currently having enacted some form of a sympathy/apology law.
- However, no law is needed for a physician to show empathy or even apologize.
- Cover-ups and service lapses after adverse events spur litigation and severity, while an honest defendant takes the wind out of a case.
- Apology and disclosure must be "done right" under the auspices of a program to avoid hurried or botched apologies, which can be misinterpreted.

CHAPTER 8
THIS IS A JOB FOR PATIENTS TOO!

There can be little doubt that the real winners of the disclosure programs are patients and their families. One can only imagine (Doug's family does not have to) the cascade of emotions when things go wrong. All of us place tremendous faith in our healthcare professionals. For good reason. We are blessed with healthcare professionals with tremendous talent, and for the overwhelming majority, individuals who are compassionate, caring, well educated, experienced, and "driven for the right reasons." When we go to them as patients, our hopes, dreams, and expectations are all sky high. Psychologists have shared with us that patients and their families, in the present day environment, almost never envision their surgery, their treatment regime, or their test not going right. They have heard of complications, but they do not imagine it could happen to them! Even with effective informed consent, no patient thinks that they will be the statistic that is reviewed with them. An actual error is even more remote in their mind. When either happens, it is a crushing realization. The procedure that they have been waiting months for, having endured a tremendous amount of pain, hoping that conservative therapy would work, taking time off from work for this one procedure to make the pain go away … causes them to be in worse shape than when they started! It happens. And it certainly happens notwithstanding the fact that the health care professionals had provided appropriate and even excellent care. But that does not make the continued pain and the expense that the patient is going to incur any better. Psychologists tell us this is a double whammy for patients. Not only are they left with an unfortunate medical or physical circumstance, they are also in emotional turmoil. The individual whom they trusted literally with their life let them down. The individual with whom they had a trusting relationship has breached that trust. Can they trust you further? Will you be honest about what happened? Patients and their families sadly become suspicious. During that period of time when they actually need you more than ever, there is a tendency from the patients to pull away. Unfortunately, their family members and well-wishers can inadvertently help in this negative process. In other words, instead of telling the patient to head back first to the doctor, they feed the suspicion and suggest that they visit "their cousin Vinny!"

We know, post-adverse event, that patients need, more than anything else, their doctor. They need additional support, information, someone to answer their questions and concerns, and someone to hear their frustrations. There is no one better to fill this role than their doctor. If patients stay connected with their doctor, he or she can explain to them what occurred. They can review with the patient again why they feel a complication occurred, if they know. Focus on what they are going to do next. Allay their suspicions. If a true mistake has occurred, the patient needs to know why, to the extent that question can be answered. The patient will want to know what is going to be done to reduce the potential of such a mistake happening again, and the patient will want to be treated fairly. Patients should not have to engage a lawyer simply to find out the information that they badly need and deserve. Patients should not have to engage a lawyer to initiate a lawsuit and go through three or four years of litigation if they are entitled to compensation. The lack of a process that we have referred to as "event management" (see chapter 4) is a gaping hole in our efforts to support patients' and doctors' efforts to maintain solid relationships. *Let's be clear … when there is an unfortunate or even tragic outcome … patients need to go back to their doctor, at least first!*

Patients should be encouraged to return to their providers, first.

The litigation process is hard certainly on the doctor, but in an underrealized way, it is extraordinarily hard on the patient and the family. You heard bits of that in chapter 1 from Doug. Can any of us imagine having to be cross-examined on the worst tragedy of our lives? Many have said that their deposition in which they were challenged about what occurred (in some cases actually blaming the patient or family members) is even worse than the incident itself. The litigation process is long and difficult. It includes drafting a complaint that, of course, the patient's counsel would do, but must be reviewed in detail by the patient; responding to discovery; giving up a lot of one's right to privacy; participating in often long depositions; having to review information that is provided by the doctor's counsel; and often, if it gets to a trial, taking between a week and two weeks, sometimes more, to have the case heard by a jury.

Imagine, as a patient, going through that entire process just to have the jury indicate that they do not feel the doctor was responsible. Various statistics show that physicians win approximately 85% of these cases that go to trial. One can only imagine the lasting effects of having a jury of *your* (the patient's) peers disagree with these allegations that you (the patient) have come to sincerely believe and live with over several years. It is going to not only open the wound, but perhaps sadly prevent it from healing — indefinitely.

Now, let's look at what would happen if we acted in accord with the concepts described earlier in this book. The patient and the family would receive immediate support from their healthcare team. They would receive information about what had occurred and assurances of what is being done to prevent it from occurring again. If compensation was due, they would receive it in perhaps months instead of years (if at all). Of course, there will be good faith differences of opinion, but when everyone is talking, it becomes a small subset. The key is rather obvious, but understated and under-realized! We have quite a different process when we all work together.

For this process to work, both sides of the equation need to be present, with an acceptance by healthcare professionals of the theories and the strategies described in this book, which we are happy to say, has begun to occur around the country and will continue. However, patients must give their doctors a chance. Patients must go back to their doctor at least first. All too often a doctor reaches out only to find that a patient's lawyer has instructed them not to communicate. When this happens, everyone loses.

Perhaps a grassroots campaign is needed. Perhaps medical societies across the country need to reach out to the patient population and let them know that their doctor is there for them, even when these unfortunate, terrible adverse events occur. Maybe this chapter needs to be in every reception area so that patients know that although medical errors and complications are rare, they do happen. When they do, the relationship should not fracture. We need to stay on the same side of the table, the doctor and the patient, even when expectations are not met or a complication occurs. This has been a recurring theme in this book. There is perhaps no more important fundamental concept. Let's get the word out so we can spread this concept. Let's put it on our website; let's be creative on how we get this positive message out. Of course, it is uncomfortable to discuss "what we do when things go wrong," but years ago healthcare professionals were uncomfortable about discussing informed consent. Now it has become a standard part of patient education. Can we fit in a statement about talking to your doctor *if* a complication occurs? Perhaps it is a first step.

The point is that the concept of Sorry Works! and disclosure have always been focused on what the doctor should do and what the doctor's responsibilities entail. Those clearly are important, but let's be clear about the patient and family responsibilities too. Patients should resist the temptation that one must retain counsel immediately. In some subset of cases, of course, it may become necessary, but often that is not the case. Even when counsel is involved, it does not have to mean that there are three or four years of contentious and expensive litigation. Your attorney authors have dealt with many very fine plaintiff's lawyers through a disclosure process sometimes resulting in payments and sometimes not. Let's at least start on the same side of the table!

Review Points:

- Patients and their families are the true winners of a disclosure program.
- When an adverse event occurs, patients need to go back to their doctors first!
- A grassroots campaign is needed!

CHAPTER 9

THE REALIZED BENEFITS OF
DISCLOSURE SUCCESS STORIES

Lexington, Massachusetts, is the site of the famous "shot heard 'round the world'" that opened the American Revolution against King George. Lexington, *Kentucky*, is the site of the "shot heard 'round the medical malpractice world.'" To be fair, Dr. Steve Kraman and Ginny Hamm, JD, of the Lexington Veterans Affairs Hospital did not set out to be revolutionaries. They just wanted to develop a better way to treat patients and families after adverse medical events. However, their work has left a legacy that has truly sparked a revolution within healthcare, insurance, and legal fields. The Sorry Works! message was initially modeled after their disclosure program, and Dr. Kraman serves on the board of The Sorry Works! Coalition.

The Lexington Veterans Affair lost two major lawsuits in the early 1980's. Significant sums of money were lost (both in the verdicts and litigation expenses), but more importantly, doctors and patients/families turned into bitter enemies during the litigation process. It was not the way they wanted to run a hospital. So, Dr. Kraman and Ms. Hamm developed a system to quickly identify bad outcomes so they would not be blindsided by lawsuits.

One of the first cases they identified involved the death of a woman who entered the Lexington Veterans' Affairs Hospital with several health complications. The woman's daughters did not suspect anything — their mom was in poor health — and they had her body picked up from the hospital and prepared for burial with no questions asked. However, the woman's death was unexpected, and the hospital staff did a thorough investigation. As it turned out, the investigation found that errors hastened the woman's death. This was a telling moment, because here was a case that could have been easily swept under the rug. The daughters thought it was Mom's time and no attorneys would have been banging down the door. But what is the definition of character? Doing the right thing when no one is watching.

The Lexington VA officials called the daughters and informed them that they had some information to share about their mother's death. The daughters were advised to retain legal counsel, and a meeting was scheduled. In that meeting, Dr. Kraman and his colleagues apologized, admitted fault, explained what happened, and discussed compensation. The case was settled in a few weeks.

The skeptic might say, *"Well, that's a great story, but no wonder the federal government is in debt up to its eyeballs...These guys are handing out money like it's water!"*

Not true. The experience from the woman's death led to the creation of a disclosure program at the Lexington VA in 1987. After seven years of a disclosure program, the Lexington VA, when compared to 35 other similarly-situated VA facilities, was in the top quartile for total claims — because they were disclosing so much — but they were in the bottom quartile for total payments. Over a 13-year period, the program handled over 170 claims, and the largest single payment made was $341,000 for a wrongful death case. According to data from the office of the VA general counsel, in the year 2000, the mean national VA malpractice judgment was $413,000, the mean settlement pre-trial was $98,000, and the mean settlement at trial was $248,615. During that same year (2000), Lexington's mean payment was $36,000.[33]

In fall 2005, the U.S. Department of Veterans Affairs mandated that all of their facilities follow Lexington's lead by implementing disclosure programs.[34]

The skeptic might counter, *"Well, these numbers are fine and the VA should be applauded for mandating this approach system-wide, but we have to remember that this involves a government hospital where cases are adjudicated in the federal court system. This program will never work in our community hospital that has to deal with the daily realities of unpredictable local judges and juries."*

Critics who make this argument fail to understand a basic precept of Sorry Works — this program is about patients and families and controlling anger, not about lawyers, judges, or the courts. When *customers* enter a healthcare facility, be it government, private self-insured, or a community hospital, they enter with the same hopes, expectations, and fears. Patients are patients, families are families, *customers* are *customers*, no matter where they get their care. And if *customers* smell a cover-up after an adverse medical event, they will become angry, no matter what type of hospital is shutting them out. Controlling anger is the reason the Lexington VA was in the lowest quartile for total payments despite being in the highest quartile for claims. They removed anger from the process and in so doing removed customers' desire to financially punish the institution. Anger, not greed, is what drives severity. True, it is easier to establish a disclosure program in a government facility, but the perceived barriers of doing so in community hospitals can be overcome.

> "Controlling anger is the reason the Lexington VA was in the lowest quartile for total payments despite being in the highest quartile for claims. They removed anger from the process and in so doing removed customers' desire to financially punish the institution. Anger, not greed, is what drives severity."

It took some time, but disclosure programs began to appear at organizations outside the VA system. Early programs continue to exist, and successes have been reported. This chapter will review the many successful disclosure programs that have been implemented across the country.

University of Michigan Health System. Perhaps one of the most well-known disclosure programs is the one adopted by the University of Michigan (UM) Health System in 2001. Its program is similar in scope and intent to the Lexington program — however, UM's program has an interesting twist. When starting the program, UM staff told trial lawyers who typically sued their system about the program.[35] UM leadership pledged to catch medical errors while patients/families were still under their care and deal fairly with patient/families and their legal counsel. However, UM conceded they were not going to catch every error before a patient/family left their facility, and sometimes medical complications surface days, weeks, months, and even years down the road. UM asked the Michigan trial bar, when people showed up in their offices asking to sue UM, that they (the trial bar), contact UM before filing any paperwork with the courts. UM pledged to meet with trial lawyers in such cases, and if legitimate errors were apparent, settle quickly and fairly. If, however, the complaints were without merit, UM would never settle such cases.

UM's results are extremely promising. Claims are down from 262 cases in 2001 to less than 100 cases in 2006 (back to pre-1990 levels). Reserves have been cut from $72 million to less than $20 million, and transaction expenses have been reduced from $48,000 per case to $21,000 per case. Finally, closings for cases have decreased from an average of 20.3 months to 9.5 months.[36]

In addition to good numbers, UM is changing the culture of medicine and law in the Wolverine State. When the disclosure program started in 2001, the majority of the UM medical staff were suspicious and apprehensive. Five years later, 98% of the UM medical staff support the program, and 55% said the program was a "significant factor" to stay at UM.[37] The UM disclosure program has become a retention program too — fascinating!

The Michigan trial bar is also responding in a positive fashion. Seventy-one percent said the program is leading them to settle cases for less; 81% said costs are less, and 57% said they are passing on cases they would have tried in the past.[38] Trial lawyers are saying that since the UM system is honest in their dealings, the good feelings are being reciprocated.

News flash for the medical and insurance communities: Trial lawyers are human beings! Their clients are human beings too. If you treat people with respect, the respect will be returned. If you treat people poorly, the disrespect will be returned. UM has accomplished in six years what 40 years of tort reform has failed to do: Change the behavior of the trial bar. Instead of trying to bludgeon the trial bar, perhaps the medical and insurance communities should learn to treat trial lawyers with respect and professional dignity and see what happens. You might be surprised!

Like the VA program, UM's program is based on three simple principles:[39]

1) Apologize and compensate quickly and fairly when medical care causes injury;
2) Defend medically appropriate care vigorously; and
3) Learn from mistakes so they are not repeated, further reducing liability exposure.

It is hard for anyone to disagree with these principles. Point #2 is extremely important. UM's program is *not* a no-fault compensation scheme. Well-meaning people often believe that disclosure programs are simply saying sorry all the time with an open checkbook. No! Adverse medical events where a thorough investigation shows the standard of care was met will *not* result in compensation to the patient or family. In such cases, the medical providers will empathize with the patient/family and their legal counsel, answer questions, share records, and dispel any notion of a cover-up while proving their innocence, but no settlement will be offered or approved — ever. Furthermore, if a lawsuit is initiated, the case will be aggressively defended to jury verdict. Healthcare professionals are never sold out in a Sorry Works! disclosure program. In fact, for disclosure programs to be successfully implemented, the medical staff has to know they will backed up when they do their job. Many healthcare providers find this approach refreshing. Alternatively, cases of obvious negligence are settled quickly and fairly, saving everyone time, money, and stress while providing the healing all sides need (healthcare professionals included). Indeed, disclosure programs such as Sorry Works! turn the world of medical malpractice litigation on its

> "…for disclosure programs to be successfully implemented the medical staff has to know they will backed up when they do their job."

head! Providers who have done their job are never forced to settle a claim, while patients and families who have legitimate injuries (be they large *or* small) do not have to wait years for justice.

University of Illinois Medical Center. In 2006, the University of Illinois Medical Center in Chicago developed a disclosure program based on the Michigan approach. In developing its disclosure principles, the University of Illinois adopted the three Michigan principles listed above and added a new one:

1) We will provide effective communication to patients and families following adverse patient events.
2) Apologize and compensate quickly and fairly when medical care causes injury.
3) Defend medically appropriate care vigorously.
4) Learn from mistakes so they are not repeated, further reducing liability exposure.

In the program's first year, 40 disclosures were made, but only one claim was filed. **Please note:** The University of Illinois Medical Center operates in Cook County, Illinois, which, according to the American Tort Reform Association, in 2006 was the fourth-worst judicial hellhole in the United States.[40] If a disclosure program can work in this litigation climate, it can work *anywhere*.

There are other unique elements of the University of Illinois Medical Center disclosure program that are worth noting:[41]

> **The University of Illinois Medical Center operates in Cook County, Illinois, which, according to the American Tort Reform Association, in 2006 was the fourth-worst judicial hellhole in the United States. If a disclosure program can work in this litigation climate, it can work *anywhere*.**

- UI tries to conduct all investigations into adverse events within 72 hours or less, and their goal is to disclose, apologize, and settle all matters in 60 days or less. They have a rapid investigation team as well as a disclosure team trained in communicating bad news to patients and families.
- The biggest barrier faced by UI in establishing their program was outside defense counsel. According to Dr. Tim McDonald, leader of the UI disclosure program, when UI was starting their disclosure program the medical center was also interviewing for new outside counsel. During interviews, a question was posed to the prospective attorneys how they would handle a surgery where the wrong leg was removed. Twelve of the 16 firms counseled deny and defend, and one even advocated altering the medical record to imply that the "wrong leg" needed to be removed anyway! Amazing. Dr. McDonald said you have to hire defense counsel who will accept litigating cases before the courts only on damages.
- Dr. McDonald has shared several moving stories about the UI disclosure program, including an event where a patient was given a massive overdose of cancer-fighting drugs. The patient was in

excruciating pain and bleeding everywhere. The providers sat on the incident for a few days and felt horrible. Some of the providers involved in the incident became physically ill, while others could not sleep. However, McDonald's team learned about the event, investigated quickly, and organized a disclosure meeting. The patient could not believe the honesty and candor. She was so glad to hear that she would not be sick anymore and that her illness was not the cause of the problem. Furthermore, she was pleased the mistake was identified and corrected so it would not happen to another patient. Finally, her bills were waived, which pleased her too. As for the providers, they got a huge load of their chest and felt so much better afterwards. It's all about healing!

- Billing is part of the UI disclosure program. With one keystroke all billing is stopped to a patient/family after an adverse event. This is an important point, because often an errant bill or collection notice sent to a patient or family can significantly hurt the relationship. Regulatory billing issues must be discussed with counsel.

- UI also has a patient liaison to continually work with patients/families and make sure they never feel abandoned after adverse events.

Catholic Healthcare West. The July 2007 edition of *Las Vegas Life* reported the following on the Catholic Healthcare West disclosure program:

> "....Catholic Healthcare West, which operates hospitals in Arizona, California, and Nevada (including St. Rose Dominican Hospitals), instituted a full-disclosure program in 2002. Mike Tymczyn, vice president of communications for St. Rose, said the numbers were encouraging. "Although Catholic Healthcare West cannot for certain link the implementation of the full-disclosure program (to a drop in claims), there has been an overall decrease in claims since that time," Tymczyn said. "It's not an exact correlation, because of the way claims are reported, but there has been a decrease."[42]

COPIC. COPIC Insurance is a doctor-owned insurance company based in Colorado that has operated a disclosure/early offer program since 2000. It has been reported that COPIC's 3Rs program has cut malpractice claims against physicians participating in the program by 50% and reduced settlement costs by 23%[43]

COPIC does have some serious deviations from the Sorry Works! approach, though, that should be noted. The 3Rs program — which stands for "Recognize, Respond, and Resolve" — is a no-fault system. Furthermore, cases involving deaths are not handled by the 3Rs program. Finally, patients and families cannot be represented by legal counsel nor can there by any written demands for compensation.[44] However, patients and families are not required to sign a waiver of further liability if they accept money from COPIC, preserving their right to file a lawsuit if they still wish. COPIC's theory (and hope) is that patients and families will no longer be angry after completing the program and will forego litigation, even though the option is still available to them. They report positive results. The program has made payments to over 900 injured patients since 2000. Cases in the 3Rs program have settled on average for $5,300 versus non-3Rs closed cases, which settled for $88,056 in 2003, $74,643 in 2004, and $77,936 in 2005.[45]

COPIC's successes have been with smaller cases (usually $30,000 or less in value). It has been reported that they have not been able to get cases larger in value through the program. The failure of the 3Rs program to attract larger cases is easy to understand: Patients and families with life-changing injuries or wrongful deaths want their own legal counsel to ensure they are being treated fairly. 3Rs says attorneys are not welcome, so these patients and families opt for traditional litigation, which costs everyone enormous sums of time and money. Severely injured patients or families dealing with wrongful death cases are simply not going to trust the insurance company to act in their best interest… they are going to want their own attorney to speak for them. Remember, successful disclosure programs focus on what the *customers* want!

Despite these important differences, COPIC's program shares many philosophical beliefs with Sorry Works! chiefly that anger is what drives patients and families to file medical malpractice lawsuits. Like Sorry Works! COPIC believes that improved communication focused on solving problems and maintaining relationships between healthcare providers and patients/ families is the key to controlling liability exposure.

The most critical element of the COPIC success story is that it shows that an insurance company can implement a disclosure and early-offer program that reduces lawsuits and costs by mitigating anger felt by patients and families.

Other Programs. There are countless other hospitals, small healthcare institutions (such as Lasik and orthopaedic surgery centers), and insurance groups that are practicing disclosure and early offer programs — albeit quietly; for example, one alternative insurance vehicle in central Pennsylvania, Central Pennsylvania Physicians Risk Retention Group, which insures nearly 1,200 healthcare professionals in a nine-county region in Pennsylvania. Its risk management program has adopted the concept of apology and disclosure and works with its physicians as adverse events arise to appropriately manage events. Physicians are educated and counseled on the disclosure concept. When appropriate, claims are placed on fast track, providing quick closure to patients, their families, and physicians as well as reducing litigation reserves and expenses. Early results of this young program (five years) are showing successes!

Other publicized programs include:

- Stanford University Teaching Hospitals has a disclosure and early-offer program.[46]
- Harvard Teaching Hospitals are developing a program.[47]
- Twenty-eight different Kaiser hospitals operating an early-offer compensation program similar to Sorry Works! report positive changes in their liability exposure as well.[48]
- Children's Hospitals and Clinics of Minnesota — operating in a state without tort reform and treating children (i.e., huge liability exposure) — is successfully operating a disclosure program.[49]
- In 2001, Johns Hopkins Hospital adopted an apology and disclosure program.

The early data is simply too compelling for healthcare and insurance professionals and their companies not to embrace apology and disclosure. We can learn from the early programs and early successes. We know far more now than we did a decade ago. We can bring physicians, risk managers, administrators, staff, and other healthcare providers on-board to the concept, and we can execute a program that works effectively to strengthen patient relationships and better an organization's bottom line. We can take what has been learned and even develop disclosure programs that climb to the next level, combining expanded informed consent and patient accountability with enhanced post-event communication and alternative dispute resolution.[50] We can really begin to attack this liability equation and do something good for doctors and patients all at the same time!

Review Points:

- Disclosure and apology programs in hospitals and insurance companies have shown early successes!
- Disclosure and apology programs can help organizations financially at the same time that they strengthen the physician-patient relationship.

QUESTIONS & CHALLENGES
IN CONTEXT

The most common questions and challenges to "I'm sorry," apology, and disclosure are addressed below. Of course, every question is fact-specific, so in this context, we have simply tried to cover general concepts. However, these general concepts will certainly give you a start and be especially helpful in handling doubters and naysayers. Furthermore, the authors are happy to respond to additional questions or challenges. We do it all the time!

QUESTION	*OK, we agree with disclosure, including the part about compensating patients and families injured by our errors. But how do you determine what is fair compensation?*
ANSWER:	You are describing an event that, after due diligence, you have determined was a breach of the standard of care and causally related; a medication error, for example, where harm is causally connected and substantiated. Your team should reach out early and involve your insurer, if commercially insured, or if self-insured, the risk manager who may be the individual who handles your claims. The risk manager may be on the disclosure team. Valuing the damages is always difficult. The key is to diffuse the anger. A couple of suggestions follow. Look to meet needs: Missed work, transportation expenses, waiver of bills under certain circumstances, and/or payment of subsequent expenses. Think about noneconomic activities that often are meaningful, such as a lecture series on safety or a certain aspect of training to show the patient/family you are improving your processes so the mistake does not happen again (a very important point for many patients and families who have suffered medical errors). As to the exact offer, rely on your claims personnel who has experience in these matters, but do not resort to the *"Let's low ball and see if they take it."* Obviously, the amount is going to be less if counsel is not involved, but it

must be in the fair range to be credible (and to ensure the long-term credibility of your program). You will present an offer, and then typically the patient/family and their attorney — if they are represented — will counteroffer. It is a process. The key, however, is that it is not done with anger and spite...which often are the key drivers of escalating damages.

QUESTION   *As a surgical group, although our quality is quite high, clearly complications occur and, at times, unfortunately, even mistakes. Many of us have always wanted to reach out quickly to patients, but our insurer has discouraged the same. How does this work? Do we establish our own fund for these early payments? Where does the money come from?*

ANSWER: The compensation paid should normally come from your insurance carrier, and this is why we say to collaborate with your insurance carrier early on. Many enlightened carriers are willing to make a small payment pre-suit, and they will even entertain paying a large claim if warranted and if due diligence has been accomplished. Of course, for most claims insurers will want a general release executed. The topic of a general release can be worked into your discussions with patients and their families, and you may find that the inclusion of plaintiff's counsel may make this part of this process proceed more smoothly. However, if your particular insurer is not interested in an early intervention where appropriate, you ought to tell them about concepts such as disclosure and what is being discussed by Sorry Works! because if they are not interested in a collaborative disclosure program, they may not be doing all they can for you as an insured. Further, in fact many physicians are starting their own self-funded plans or captive insurance programs. Some of the most successful insurance vehicles are what is commonly referred to as risk retention groups. You may be interested to know that the so-called alternative risk financing market (insurance vehicles other than the traditional commercial carriers) now provide insurance for more than half of the healthcare market. Perhaps they are no longer the alternative? However, the dollars often will come from your self-funded program (captive) or from your insurance carrier. The key is early collaboration. Finally, there are decisions to be made about whether or not an individual physician wants their insurance carrier to pay, because it raises National Practitioner Databank questions. This is something legal counsel meeting with the doctor will review as there are certain legal requirements that will need to be considered. In the end, if your insurance company is not on-board with the Sorry Works! concept, perhaps it is time to shop for insurance.

CHALLENGE: *Doctors will become sitting ducks with Sorry Works!. They will get their pants sued off.*

RESPONSE: After having read the nine chapters in this book, you know this statement is false. Severity is often the product of adverse evidence created either from a service lapse, a lack of communication, or poor communication post-adverse event — not by physicians being honest and open. *Sorry Works!* works 100% of the time. If one does not completely understand the difference between showing empathy and enhanced communication and an actual apology accepting responsibility, you could then inadvertently miscommunicate (see chapter 2). However, this is why we emphasize having a disclosure educational program, a disclosure policy, and a disclosure program so that the entire team understands how to appropriately integrate this powerful concept.

CHALLENGE: *What if "I'm sorry" doesn't work? Hasn't a doctor just admitted guilt? Isn't this going to be problematic in court?*

RESPONSE: Again, one must understand the difference between saying, "I'm sorry," and accepting responsibility. Remember, "I'm sorry" is an expression of empathy. An apology includes acceptance of responsibility. The key is placing "I'm sorry" in context. Certainly, saying, "I'm sorry," for a complication or an unfortunate outcome is not going to put you in harm's way in the court, particularly if you learn simple steps and concepts concerning the same. Even an apology that includes acceptance of responsibility, assuming it is done *after* appropriate due diligence, is also not going to hurt you in the courtroom either. You have already determined that this is a case in which responsibility lies at your feet. These are cases in all likelihood that should be fast-tracked in claims, and all effort should be made to reach a fair resolution prior to a lawsuit being initiated. However, resolution is not always possible because the parties can honestly disagree on the value of a claim. Under such circumstances, the claim has to move forward, but often for simply an evaluation of the damages. There are cases that are argued quite successfully in court on just damages with plaintiffs receiving far less than what is offered to them in the first place. When we say far less we mean literally less, which means that the plaintiff's attorney and unfortunately his or her client have truly gone in reverse. To pursue a claim on damages plaintiffs may have to invest $40,000 to $50,000 or more in expenses and years of their own time and effort, all to sometimes receive a judgment less than they could have obtained very early on. Accepting responsibility for something you are responsible for, in collaboration with your insurer, should help you in the courtroom, not hinder you.

QUESTION: *Who makes disclosure or apology in most disclosure programs? Is it the doctor, nurse, or hospital administrator? What if the doctor is not a good communicator?*

ANSWER: Determining the right communicator is part of implementing a disclosure program. As discussed in previous chapters, you will have a disclosure team. The disclosure team members need to decide who is best positioned to disclose to the patient and family. It almost always involves the provider with some coaching and help from the disclosure team. However, if the provider is a poor communicator and/or the relationship with the patient/family is severely strained, then the disclosure team may completely take over the disclosure process, or it may be that a colleague, nurse, patient safety officer, or risk manager is the most sensible substitute for the provider. Disclosure literally needs to be evaluated on a case-by-case basis.

QUESTION: *What circumstances require disclosure? Is there any standard? What about situations where there has been an error but no apparent injury, such as a medication error? Perhaps this is better off left unsaid?*

ANSWER: The answers to these questions are somewhat dependent on state law. However, the general rule is that if an error reaches a patient, disclosure is appropriate, **whether or not there is an injury.** You have to think of this from the family/patient's perspective and whether or not they would want to receive the information. In almost all circumstances they will. There have been circumstances where doctors have placed their judgment in place of the patient, convincing themselves that no damage occurred and disclosing the medical error would simply alarm the family. However, the family often will find out about the medical error from a third party. Now we have the anger and distrust that we have worked hard to prevent; that same anger that leads patients and/or families to attorneys.

QUESTION: *Our hospital has a disclosure policy in place, but how do we get a disclosure program started?*

ANSWER: As mentioned in chapter 5, having a disclosure policy is important, and many hospitals, pursuant to JCAHO Standards,[51] have adopted disclosure policies in the last several years. However, the true home run is making sure you have a disclosure *program*. This means buy-in to the concept at the most senior level and then literally making sure it takes place on the front line when an adverse event occurs. Following the steps set forth in chapter 5 will help. Starting with education is always critical. This is really an issue of culture. Showing empathy, enhanced communication, and five-star service are issues that sound good but are difficult to consistently apply in the demanding pace our healthcare professionals find themselves. Therefore, if you have a policy, that is a great place to start. Now see if you can transcend that policy to a true program.

QUESTION: *If, pursuant to our disclosure policy and program, we go through each step and offer, for example, $300,000, but the patient and her lawyer counteroffer with $1 million, what do we do then?*

ANSWER: As mentioned in previous chapters, there are cases in which there will be true disagreement on the question of value. However, if you have done what you can to diffuse the anger and the emotional components of the claim and put yourself in the best light possible, these cases are ripe for what is commonly referred to as a mediation. This means getting a neutral third party to hear both sides of the story and determine what the value of the potential claim may be. Often it was thought that only lawsuits are mediated. Clearly, even in the pre-suit stages, mediation can get you to a number both sides can agree on. Often, it is a number that both sides are not complete happy with ... but happier than moving forward!

CHALLENGE: *Lawyers simply file too many lawsuits in my hometown for disclosure to be successful here.*

RESPONSE: If a region or county is considered to be friendly to plaintiffs' attorneys, it is an area ripe for a disclosure program. Doctors, hospital administrators, and insurers should do everything possible to make sure that patients and families do not leave their offices angry in litigious regions and prevent them from getting to the plaintiff attorney's office in the first place. A disclosure program provides the protocol and methods to alleviate anger and significantly diminish the chances of lawsuits being filed, especially in the most litigious areas. An overly aggressive trial attorney is powerless without an angry, yet sympathetic plaintiff.

CHALLENGE: *But not all bad medical outcomes are the result of errors. Sometimes people just die or are injured despite the best efforts of a medical staff. We can't be handing out checks every time someone dies or doesn't heal completely.*

RESPONSE: You are absolutely correct. Many times the standard of care is met, but people still die or do not completely heal. Doctors and hospitals certainly should not be expected to "hand out checks" under such circumstances, nor should they be expected to deliver an apology that includes an admission of fault or wrongdoing. However, providers still need to communicate with patients and families in an empathetic fashion (*"We are sorry this happened."*). Lack of communication and empathy as well as a perception of a cover-up produces lawsuits even when the standard of care was met. Again, it is understanding the difference between saying, "I'm sorry," and accepting responsibility.

Disclosure programs like Sorry Works! stress communication with patients and families, including in circumstances when an error did NOT occur. They are perhaps most important under these circumstances. Medical staff and administrators should make themselves available to answer questions, provide insight, and empathize with the patient and family — do everything you can to appear honest and transparent ... and be so! But a settlement is not required when no error occurred. If the patient or family attempts to file a lawsuit, the hospital must be clear that it will defend itself vigorously and not settle. This is where your disclosure program pays dividends. Hospitals that practice the Sorry Works! concept develop a reputation for honesty with local plaintiff's attorneys. If the hospital plans to contest a case (no settlement), local attorneys learn that such cases are probably without merit and not worth pursuing. We call this effect "The Honesty Dividend."

CHALLENGE: *What about "bad-baby cases?" Surely disclosure cannot work for OB/GYNs.*

RESPONSE: Sure it can. There is no question that the so-called tragic "bad-baby" cases are emotional and financially significant and actually speak to larger societal issues (and problems), but Sorry Works! is an excellent way to begin addressing this situation. Every birth with unexpected outcomes or adverse events should be met head-on with excellent customer service and outstanding communication. Such cases will literally test the communication and customer service principles of your disclosure program.

There is no question that bad-baby cases where no error occurred still often result in litigation because the parents have no other financial options to pay for the care of a neurologically impaired child. Some parents are faced with financial ruin, so they try to file a lawsuit. These cases must be tried on the medicine and science. However, evidence of good communication post-adverse event will also be essential to your defense. Remember, you are being opposed by extremely sympathetic plaintiffs. You can have science on your side, but if communication was not appropriate the "plus" will be created. If so, insurer/doctor/hospital will feel forced to settle.

CHALLENGE: *I'm OK disclosing to a patient or their family and even discussing compensation if we caused injury or death, but if they bring legal counsel then the meeting is canceled. All bets will be off.*

RESPONSE: Lawyers can be helpful with the process. You should not stop the process, but you do need to involve your counsel. In this regard, make sure you have counsel who understands what is going to be accomplished, including the potential of arguing the case only on the damages in court should a resolution be unattainable. The disclosure process should not turn into *counsel* taking the lead; it is still between you and the patient. Think of this as the opportunity not only to make things right with the patient, but also to convince plaintiff counsel that either your offer is fair and reasonable or no case exists. If you do not meet, a lawsuit will often result.

QUESTION: *What if my insurance company says "no" to implementing a Sorry Works! program? What should I do then?*

ANSWER: Change their mind or fire them! Doctors and hospitals are customers of insurance companies, and as customers you need to tell your insurer that disclosure programs are in keeping with your culture and you see the value. Make phone calls, send e-mails, write letters, and get other colleagues involved. It's your hospital ... your practice ... your patients and families... Take control by demanding Sorry Works! If the insurer digs their heels in, it is probably a lack of knowledge or a culture that is not a good fit with yours.

QUESTION: *What exactly does Sorry Works! advocate in terms of the timing of disclosure? The investigation may take weeks to months, and on the basis of that analysis one decides whether the standard of care was met and then discloses accordingly. It strikes me that there are situations where even from the get-go you know the adverse event was due to error, for example, wrong site surgery. At this point in time, that would consistently fall below the standard of care. Can you advise as to timing of disclosure? It seems unreasonable to wait a few weeks for the details when the error is so blatant and obvious. What about this situation?*

ANSWER: You are correct. Cases where gross/obvious errors happened need to move a little more quickly; however, not too quickly. After an obvious error (say a wrong-site surgery, as you reference), the patient/family needs to know that an error happened, that you are sorry, and that you/your staff are going to evaluate and determine what happened and will share this information with them. But do not assign blame to individuals or systems — yet. Instead, focus on attending to the immediate needs of the patient/family (food, assistance with phone calls, bills, lodging), give them your contact information, and answer any calls or inquiries for information quickly and friendly. Do not ever give a patient or family any reason to suspect a cover-up. Stay on the same side of the table.

You need to do a complete evaluation and learn exactly what happened, who was involved, how the mistake occurred, and how the problem(s) will be fixed so that the potential for a similar error is reduced. You should, however, keep the family/patient informed as the investigation continues. You do not want them to think that you are doing nothing or are just putting them off. After you have gathered this information, recontact the patient/family and tell them you want to schedule a meeting. In the second meeting, you will explain everything that happened, apologize, and accept responsibility and continue discussions about their needs. This will lead to a discussion about settlement and a number. Expect, as mentioned before, for there to be some back and forth.

QUESTION: *At what point do you initiate conversations regarding compensation? Do you come prepared to offer compensation at the time of full disclosure? If so, how do you evaluate for damages if you don't have information regarding wages, children, etc.?*

ANSWER: The very first disclosure meeting usually happens in the immediate aftermath of the event. Go to the family or patient and tell them something has happened. Empathize ("We are sorry this happened .... we feel very badly for you and your family"). Attend to their immediate needs, let them know you will do a quick and thorough investigation, and promise to get back to them at a certain date. Provide contact information for them (do not ever let them feel abandoned ... they must feel connected to the facility and staff at all times).

If the investigation shows there was an error, then you need to consider compensation. However, understand that there are four elements to effective apology and disclosure after a legitimate medical error causally connected to sustained damages: 1) "sorry" or apology; 2) admission of fault; 3) explanation of what happened and how steps will be taken to prevent it from happening again; and 4) offer of fair, upfront compensation.

The four elements of disclosure and apology must generally be given in this order and may take several meetings to deliver effectively to the patient or family. The last element — compensation — may require the longest time (and several meetings) to resolve. However, if a patient or family has suffered serious financial harm due to error, they and their attorney are going to need to hear pretty quickly in the process that you intend to offer fair, upfront compensation. Then the actual amount to be paid will be determined over several meetings where you discuss and learn the actual amount of lost wages, childcare expenses, mortgage payments, and other economic factors.

Some medical providers are understandably slow in discussing compensation — some because they think it "cheapens" or degrades the disclosure event and others because they are still uncomfortable having to pay for errors. However, families and patients want to hear their economic problems are going to be addressed. If all patients and families hear at the beginning is, *"We're sorry and we'll do better next time,"* they might start to think that they are being snowed over with a phony, meaningless apology. Think about this issue from the customer perspective: *"Hey this apology is nice, but my husband can't work for six to twelve months — who is going to pay the bills and put food on the table? I guess I am going to have to sue these doctors!"*

However, you do not want to look like you are buying people off — that is completely understandable. Please understand though, when you do the first three steps sincerely (apologize, admit fault, explain) then you look very sincere and credible when you say, *"And we also intend to offer fair compensation for your injuries, and we will be discussing the amount of this compensation with you and your attorney."*

QUESTION: *If we disclose, apologize, and compensate a patient/family for an error, do we have the patient/family sign a general release? Would making a patient/family sign such a waiver anger them and reverse all the progress that has been made?*

ANSWER: Again, you have to judge each situation separately and know the players involved. Also, as part of your disclosure program, you should have discussions about such circumstances ahead of time with your insurers, attorneys, and administrators. If you are contemplating a settlement, you will often need the patient/family to sign a release. You can approach the patient/family in a way that does not anger them. It may simply be: *"Please understand. Any time one of its doctors provides compensation, my insurance company requires a release. You can have an attorney review the release before you sign it."*

QUESTION: *What role can/should nurses play in disclosure and apology?*

ANSWER: The medical malpractice crisis is to a great extent a customer service crisis — not just a legal problem. If you subscribe to this philosophy, then you should believe that nurses play a big role in disclosure and apology and an even larger role in providing excellent customer service to patients and families throughout their stay at the hospital. After all, nurses are usually the front-line employees who have the most frequent contact with the customers.

Nurses need to be educated to be on the lookout for small problems and address them quickly with good customer service. TV will not work in the patient's room? No problem — we will get a technician up to fix it right away. Food is slow coming to the patient's room? We will get the food there right away and provide a free plate with dessert for the patient's spouse. These events may sound trivial, but small problems can lead to a major blow up if an adverse event occurs. An already strained relationship may break and a lawsuit will be in the offing:

"Oh, that nurse has been so cold and uncaring. It seemed like she never answered the call button, and when she did she acted like she was doing us a favor. Now this! Something has gone wrong. I just know she and that Doctor Smith screwed up! Where's Vinny?"

Good customer service is so important and will lay the ground for successful disclosure and apology, when needed and appropriate. And nurses can lead the way!

CHALLENGE: *Sorry, but Sorry Works! is just too much of a leap of faith for the medical community.*

RESPONSE: Disclosure programs like Sorry Works! are based on data and research. It really is not hard for any of us to understand and believe. Being open and honest carefully will drive a better result and is clearly the right approach to take at this point. There are just too many success stories to doubt the economic promise of this concept. Clearly it is best for both doctors and patients.

Closing Thoughts

The litigation crisis, in part, is a customer service crisis, which can be helped by doctors, hospitals, and insurers any time — not a political problem to be solved by politicians. When doctors, hospitals, and insurance companies focus on their patients and families with excellent customer service and forget about trial lawyers, the courts, and politicians, it can bring an end to the medical malpractice crisis. Sorry Works! provides the framework to deliver excellent customer service in the minutes, hours, days, weeks, and months after an adverse medical event. **Good customer service is your new focus!**

Sorry Works! represents culture change. Turning away from deny and defend and becoming transparent and honest is a major cultural shift for medical and insurance interests. It won't happen overnight, and it won't happen without good people willing to fight the good fight. The good news is that Sorry Works! works both ethically *and* economically. The arguments waged against Sorry Works! are often emotional, knee-jerk reactions that do not hold water when examined and challenged. The key is to keep spreading and sharing information. Share this book, share the website (www.sorryworks. net), contact Stevens & Lee (jws@stevenslee.com), and share other resources about disclosure and apology. Bring speakers and trainers into your institution or organization. Take time to answer questions of well-meaning people and assuage their fears and concerns. Over time your colleagues and associates will come around and learn how sorry truly does work. **Persistent educational efforts are the key!**

In pushing for inclusion of Sorry Works! into a hospital or insurance company, settle for nothing less than a program. Obstructionists will try to appease reformers by offering policies or arguing that physicians and nurses can "do disclosure on their own." Could you imagine Disney or Southwest Airlines telling their associates to do customer service ad hoc? They wouldn't be Disney or Southwest Airlines. **Accept nothing less than a program!**

As you implement Sorry Works! and begin to experience successes, please share your success stories. The more facilities and organization that adopt disclosure and apology, the sooner reluctant institutions and individuals will begin to feel left behind. We need more people to share their success stories with trade and popular media and through personal communications with colleagues and friends. **Share your disclosure success stories!**

Thank you for reading this book, and good luck in making disclosure and apology part of the culture of your institution. The Sorry Works! Coalition and Stevens & Lee stand ready to help you with any questions or problems you may have. Call or e-mail us anytime. **You can do this, and we are here to help!**

Cheers,

Doug Wojcieszak
Founder/Spokesperson
The Sorry Works! Coalition
www.sorryworks.net
doug@sorryworks.net
618-559-8168

James W. Saxton, Esq.
Chair Healthcare Litigation
Co-Chair Health Law
Stevens & Lee
www.stevenslee.com
jws@stevenslee.com
717-399-6639

Maggie M. Finkelstein, Esq.
Stevens & Lee
mmf@stevenslee.com
717-399-6636

CME POST-READING QUIZ

<u>SORRY WORKS! DISCLOSURE, APOLOGY, AND
RELATIONSHIPS PREVENT MEDICAL MALPRACTICE CLAIMS</u>

Instructions

The post-reading quiz must be completed individually after having read *Sorry Works! Disclosure, Apology, and Relationships Prevent Medical Malpractice Claims*. The answers provided should be based on personal knowledge gained from reading the book. The quiz contains both True/False and Multiple Choice questions, and you should circle your answer directly on the quiz. There is only one correct answer. An answer key to the quiz is provided with explanations for the answers so that you can score your own quiz. You may be able to obtain CME credit for this activity. You should ensure that you follow the procedure and process required by your applicable state and/or medical society.

---

1. True or False: When you say, "I'm sorry," you are really saying, "It's my fault."

2. An overarching term for any unexpected result, bad outcome, or complication is:

    a.   Complication

    b.   Medical error

    c.   Adverse event

    d.   None of the above

3. When it comes to medical errors, patients want:

    a.   To understand what happened

    b.   An apology

    c.   To know how similar situations will be prevented in the future

    d.   All of the above

4. What drives patients to attorneys and attorneys to take on medical malpractice cases?

    a.   An adverse event coupled with an aggravating circumstance

    b.   A desire to get even

    c.   Greed

    d.   They have nothing better to do

5. By eliminating the aggravating circumstance, benefits include all of the following except:

    a.   Defense litigation expenses are reduced

    b.   Frivolous lawsuits continue

    c.   Medical errors are reduced

    d.   Better public relations

6. Event management is:

    a.   Throwing a great party

    b.   Trying to avoid a lawsuit at all costs

    c.   Your platform for a disclosure program

    d.   Not always the best method for managing adverse events

7. When an event does occur, what should you do?

    a.   Avoid the patient; no news is good news

    b.   Immediately apologize for a medical error

    c.   Let the patient know it was not your fault, but that Dr. Smith is the one to blame

    d.   Ensure the patient is safe and follow your organization's event management policy

8. Your five-step process for implementing a disclosure and apology program is:

    a.   Roll out the program to the entire organization, adopt a disclosure policy and procedure, get the decision makers on-board, train the disclosure team, and keep the program alive

    b.   Adopt a disclosure policy and procedure, get the decision makers on-board, roll out the program to the entire organization, train the disclosure team, and keep the program alive

    c.   Get the decision makers on-board, adopt a disclosure policy and procedure, roll out the program to the entire organization, train the disclosure team, and keep the program alive

    d.   Roll out the program to the entire organization, get the decision makers on-board, train the disclosure team, roll out the program to the entire organization, and keep the program alive

9. When expressing empathy, which one does not belong:

   a.   *"I'm very sorry about your loss. Please accept our condolences."*

   b.   *"I'm sorry you are feeling this way. Let me explain what happened and what we are doing to keep your care on track."*

   c.   *"These things happen all the time. In fact, it just happened to one of my other patients last week."*

   d.   *"We are sorry. We took great care to ensure your son's comfort. Let's go through his care."*

10. The three steps of disclosing a medical error include:

   a.   Empathy

   b.   Investigation

   c.   Apology and disclosure

   d.   All of the above

11. **True or False.** Physicians need a law to apologize.

12. **Which of the following is false?**

   a.   Patients and families are the true winners of a disclosure program.

   b.   When an adverse event occurs, patients need to go back to their doctors first!

   c.   A grassroots campaign is needed!

   d.   Physicians lose when it comes to disclosure.

13. **Which of the following are true?**

   a.   Early disclosure programs have not seen significant successes.

   b.   Disclosure programs can bring a financial benefit to organizations.

   c.   We can improve on the early success of disclosure programs.

   d.   Both (b) and (c).

14. Identify the correct answer to the following question: *"What if 'I'm sorry' doesn't work? Haven't I just admitted guilt? Isn't this going to be problematic in court?"*

    a.   You are right! Never say, *"I'm sorry."*

    b.   You have admitted guilt, but with the right attorney defending you, it will not be a problem in court.

    c.   Only say, *"I'm sorry,"* if you have committed a medical error; otherwise, it is not necessary.

    d.   Expressing, *"I'm sorry,"* in context will make it most effective in expressing empathy and not expressing guilt. Empathy and responsibility are different. Empathy can help you and help you in court. Not saying, *"I'm sorry,"* when it is expected can hurt you in the courtroom, in front of jurors.

15. After meeting with a patient or family after an adverse event,

    a.   Do not document the meeting. It can only be used against you later.

    b.   Do nothing more. This brings an end to this matter.

    c.   Do document the meeting and discussion in the medical record.

    d.   If you document the meeting, make sure that you put a note in about that angry brother.

CME POST-READING QUIZ
ANSWER KEY

1. False. If given context, when you say "I'm sorry," you are expressing empathy. Do not use this phrase to express fault. Reserve acceptance of responsibility for a true apology, after appropriate due diligence finding liability.

2. (c.). An overarching term for any unexpected result, bad outcome, or complication is an "adverse event." It is important to understand that an adverse event includes all medical errors and complications, but it is only when you have a medical error with liability attaching that an apology is needed. Always express empathy whether it is a complication or a medical error that has occurred.

3. (d.). According to a 2003 study in the *Journal of the American Medical Association*, patients want all of these and more, including to understand why the error occurred, how the consequences of the error will be mitigated, and disclosure of the error. (See Gallagher TH, Waterman AD, Ebers AG, Fraser VJ, and Levinson W. "Patients' and Physicians' Attitudes Regarding the Disclosure of Medical Errors." *JAMA.* 2003; 289: 1001–1007.)

4. (a.). An adverse event coupled with an aggravating circumstance. In the first instance, there must be an injury, and it is the aggravating circumstance that sends the patients running to a lawyer. It may be miscommunication by the provider to the patient, or even a complete failure to communicate with the patient, or a bad physician-patient relationship. For whatever the reason, the patient does not get the empathy and answers needed from their doctor and looks for this from an attorney. As mentioned in the book, perhaps a grassroots effort is needed to get patients to return to their doctor for answers rather than a lawyer.

5. (b.). Frivolous lawsuits can be reduced by eliminating the aggravating circumstances that lead to lawsuits in the first instance. Other benefits do include a reduction in litigation expenses, better public relations, and a reduction in medical errors.

6. (c.). Event management is your platform for a disclosure program. It is the infrastructure to support post-adverse event communication. Event management is about coordination and collaboration among healthcare professionals for the benefit of patients and healthcare providers. You should have in place an event management platform before embarking on a disclosure program.

7. (d.). Ensure the patient is safe and follow your organization's event management policy. Patient safety should always be the first priority. Implement a care plan for next steps and be sure that the patient understands the same. Your steps should also always be consistent with your organization's event management policy. Perhaps you need to notify a risk manager or your insurance company? This would be noted in your event management policy. Do not avoid the patient. It is avoidance that causes patients to fill in the gaps in the story of the care, and often, not the right information. Never place blame on another provider, particularly before any investigation and true due diligence has been completed. Likewise, you should apologize only after due diligence has determined that responsibility and liability has attached.

8. (c.). Get the decision makers on-board, adopt a disclosure policy and procedure, roll out the program to the entire organization, train the disclosure team, and keep the program alive. Following and executing these five essential steps can bring success to a disclosure program. It is essential to initially have champions who get the decision makers onboard! Before rolling out a program, work through the creation of a disclosure policy and procedure, tackle the tough questions early, and find consensus. Then move forward with rolling out the program, bringing the entire organization on-board. Identify your disclosure team and provide them with education and training. Finally, publish your successes!

9. (c.). *"These things happen all the time. In fact, it just happened to one of my other patients last week."* This phrase does not belong! All the other phrases are expressing appropriate empathy. The phrase in (c) is not empathic and makes it seem as though because what occurred now has also occurred in the past is OK. Always empathize with patients.

10. (d.). All of the above. You should always empathize with the patient/family no matter what the reason for the adverse event. It is the initial step, saying, *"I'm sorry."* Next, investigate as appropriate, following your organizational processes, to determine what happened. If an investigation reveals responsibility and fault, apologize to the patient/family and disclose what occurred, why it occurred, and how similar circumstances will be prevented in the future.

11. False. Physicians do not *need* a law to apologize. Sympathy/apology laws can be helpful, but they are not necessary. Enhanced communication post-adverse event is best for the patient/family, the healthcare provider, and the defense attorney. Apology and disclosure can help to keep the patient/family on the same side of the table and literally prevent a patient from visiting a plaintiff's lawyer.

12. (d.). Physicians are not the losers in disclosure. Physicians receive the benefit of maintaining a strong physician-patient relationship, decreased professional liability exposure, fast-tracking claims resolution, and an added emotional benefit as well.

13. (d.). Both (b) and (c). Disclosure programs can help organizations financially, reducing loss expenses and indemnity when effective; and early programs have shown success. We can improve upon these successes in the ways outlined in the book.

14. (d.). Expressing, *"I'm sorry,"* in context will make it most effective in expressing empathy and not expressing guilt. Empathy and responsibility are different. Empathy can help you and help you in court. Not saying, *"I'm sorry,"* when it is expected can hurt you in the courtroom, in front of jurors.

15. (c.). Do document the meeting and discussion in the medical record. Have this *evidence* used for you, instead of against you. Document who attended, a summary of what was discussed, next steps, who was present, the time — date — and location, and the patient understanding of what occurred and next steps.

Appendix A -

State Apology-Immunity Laws

State & Year	Citation
AZ (2005)	Ariz. Rev. Stat. Ann. §12-2605 (2005)
CA (2000)	Cal. Evid. Code § 1160 (West 2001)
CO (2003)	Colo. Rev. Stat. Ann. § 13-25-135 (West 2003)
CT (2005, as amended 2006)	Conn. Gen. Stat. Ann. §52-184d (West 2005)
DE (2006)	Del. Code Ann. tit. 10, §4318 (West 2006)
FL (2001)	Fla. Stat. Ann. §90.4026 (West 2001)
GA (2005, technical correction made 2006)	Ga. Code. Ann. §24-3-37.1 (West 2005)
HI (2007)	2007 Haw. Sess. Laws. Act 88 (H.B. 1253) (not yet codified)
ID (2006)	Idaho Code Ann. §9-207 (West 2006)
IL (2005)	735 Ill. Comp. Stat. 5/8-1901 (West 2005)
IN (2006)	Ind. Code Ann. §§ 34-43.5-1-1 to 34-43.5-1-5 (West 2006)
LA (2005)	LA. Rev. Stat. Ann. §13:3715.5 (2006)
ME (2005)	Me. Rev. Stat. Ann. tit. 24, §2907 (2005)

MD (2005)	MD. CODE. ANN., CTS. & JUD. PROC. §10-920 (West 2004)
MA (1986)	MASS. GEN. LAWS. ANN. ch. 233, §23D (West 2000)
MO (2005)	MO. ANN. STAT. §538.229 (West 2007)
MT (2005)	MONT. CODE. ANN. §26-1-814 (West 2005)
NE (2007)	2007 NEB. LAWS L.B. 373 (not yet codified)
NH (2006)	N.H. REV. STAT. ANN. §507-E:4 (2006)
NC (2004)	N.C. Gen. Stat. §8C-1, Rule 413 (West 2004)
ND (2007)	2007 N.D. H.B. 1333
OH (2004)	OHIO REV. CODE ANN. §2317.43 (LexisNexis 2007)
OK (2004)	OKLA. STAT. tit. 63, §1-1708.1H (LexisNexis 2007)
OR (2003)	OR. REV. STAT. §677.082 (2005)
SC (2006)	S.C. CODE ANN. §19-1-190 (2006)
SD (2005)	S.D. CODIFIED LAWS §19-12-14 (2007)
TN (2003)	TENN. R. EVID. RULE §409.1 (2006)
TX (1999)	TEX. CIV. PRAC. & REM. CODE ANN. §18.061 (LexisNexis 2007)
UT (2006)	UTAH CODE ANN. §78-14-18 (2007)
VT (2005)	VT. STAT. ANN. tit. 12, §1912 (2007)

VA (2005)	Va. Code Ann. §8.01-52.1 (2007)
WA (2002)	Wash. Rev. Code. §5.66.010 (2007)
WV (2005)	W. Va. Code §55-7-11a (2007)
WY (2004)	Wyo. Stat. Ann. §1-1-130 (2007)

States Not Enacted (16 states)

AL	MS
AK	NV
AR	NJ
IA	NM
KA	NY
KY	PA
MI	RI
MN	WI

APPENDIX B –

MODEL STATE LAW – DRAFT

[1] In any claim or civil action for professional negligence that is brought against a health care provider or health care facility, or in any arbitration proceeding or other method of alternative dispute resolution that relates to the claim or civil action, and in any civil or administrative proceeding against a healthcare provider or health care facility,

[2] Any written or oral statement, writing, affirmation, gesture, activity, action, or conduct, or portion thereof [could label this as any "communication" and then define "communication accordingly]

[3] [A] Expressing or conveying apology, responsibility, liability, fault, sympathy, commiseration, condolence, compassion, regret, grief, mistake, error, or a general sense of benevolence (including "sorry"), *including any accompanying explanation* ; [or include other than an expression or admission of liability or fault]

[3][B] And any offers to undertake corrective actions and gratuitous acts to assist the affected persons

[4] Made by a health care provider or employee of the health care provider [define "health care provider"]

[5] To the patient, relative of the patient, survivors of the patient, health care decision-maker for the patient, or other representative of the patient

[6] And that relates to physical loss, discomfort, pain, suffering, injury or death of the patient as the result of the unanticipated outcome of medical care [we would need to define "unanticipated outcome"]

[7] Shall be inadmissible as evidence of an admission of liability or as evidence of an admission against interest, or in any way to prove negligence or culpable conduct, and the declarant may not be examined by deposition or otherwise in proceedings about the expression or conveyance.

ENDNOTES

[1] Kraman, S., MD, and Hamm, G., JD. "Risk Management: Extreme Honesty May Be the Best Policy." *Annals of Internal Medicine.* 1999:131(12); 963-967.

[2] Boothman, R. Presentation to the New Jersey Council of Teaching Hospitals, October 2006.

[3] "Sorry." *Merriam-Webster's Online Thesaurus.* 2006–2007. http://www.m-w.com/cgi-bin/thesaurus?book=Thesaurus&va=sorry (4 Oct. 2007).

[4] "Sorry." *Merriam-Webster's Online Dictionary.* 2006–2007. http://www.m-w.com/dictionary/sorry (4 Oct. 2007).

[5] Kohn LT, et al. (eds.). "To Err is Human: Building a Safer Health System." Washington, D.C.: National Academies Press, 1999.

[6] "Error". *Merriam-Webster's Online Dictionary.* 2006–2007. http://www.m-w.com/dictionary/error (8 Oct. 2007).

[7] It is important to recognize that medical malpractice liability is state-law specific.

[8] Gallagher TH, Waterman AD, Ebers AG, Fraser VJ, and Levinson W. "Patients' and Physicians' Attitudes Regarding the Disclosure of Medical Errors." *JAMA.* 2003; 289: 1001–1007.

[9] Ibid.

[10] Kohn LT, et al. (eds.). "To Err is Human: Building a Safer Health System." Washington, D.C.: National Academies Press, 1999.

[11] "complication" *Merriam-Webster's Online Medical Dictionary.* 2006–2007. http://www.m-w.com/medical/complication (8 Oct. 2007).

[12] Hickson G, et al. "Patient Complaints and Malpractice Risk." *JAMA.* 2002; 287(22): 2951–2957; Hickson GB, Clayton EC, Githens PB, Sloan FA. "Factors that Prompted Families to File Malpractice Claims Following Perinatal Injury." *JAMA.* 1992; 287:1359–1363.

[13] Levinson W, Roter DL, Mullooly JP, Dull VT, Frankel RM. "Physician-patient Communication: The Relationship with Malpractice Claims Among Primary Care Physicians and Surgeons." *JAMA.* 1997; 277: 553–559.

[14] Witman AB, Park DM, Hardin SB. "How Do Patients Want Physicians to Handle Mistakes? A survey of internal medicine patients in an academic setting." *Arch Intern Med.* 1996; 156:2565–2569.

[15] E-mail communication with Philip H. Corboy, Attorney, Corboy & Demetrio, Oct. 19, 2007.

[16] Garrison J. "Lawyers learn to share their pain with jurors: They use a technique called psychodrama to connect better by showing vulnerability." *LA Times,* November 25, 2006.

[17] Vincent C, Young M, Phillips A. "Why Do People Sue Doctors? A Study of Patients and Relatives Taking Legal Action." *Lancet.* 1994; 343: 1609–1613.

[18] E-mail communication with Press Ganey (November 1, 2007).

[19] Ibid.

[20] JCAHO. "Ethics, Rights, and Responsibilities," in *Comprehensive Accreditation Manual for Hospitals: The Official Handbook* (Oakbrook Terrace, Ill.: JCAHO 2003), Patient Rights Standard RI. 2.90, RI-12.

[21] Perspective on Disclosure of Unanticipated Outcome Information," ASHRM whitepaper/monograph, www.ashrm.org, Nov. 2003.

[22] Boothman, R. "Apologies and a Strong Defense at the University of Michigan Health System." *The Physician Executive.* March/April 2006.

[23] Lucas S. "'Kramer' Apologizes for Racist Comments." (accessible at http://www.associatedcontent.com/article/90041/kramer_apologizes_for_racist_comments.html) (last visited October 10, 2007).

[24] "Tearful Marion Jones Apologizes, Announces Retirement." (Associated Press) (accessible at http://www.kvia.com/global/story.asp?s=7176191) (October 5, 2007; last visited October 10, 2007).

[25] Saraceno J. "Jones' Apology Sounds Like Another False Start." (accessible at http://www.usatoday.com/sports/columnist/saraceno/2007-10-07-marionjones-comment_N.htm) (last visited October 10, 2007).

[26] Lazare A. "On Apology." Oxford University Press. 2004.

[27] American Medical Association. Opinion E-8.12 Patient Information. *Code of Medical Ethics.* American Medical Association. 2006. (accessible at http://

www.ama-assn.org/ama/pub/category/8497.html) (last visited August 22, 2007).

[28] JCAHO. "Ethics, Rights, and Responsibilities," in *Comprehensive Accreditation Manual for Hospitals: The Official Handbook* (Oakbrook Terrace, Ill.: JCAHO 2003), Patient Rights Standard RI. 2.90, RI-12.

[29] MASS. GEN. LAWS ANN. ch. 233, § 23D (West 2000).

[30] Cohen JR. "Toward Candor After Medical Error: The First Apology Law." *Harvard Health Policy Rev.* 2004; 51:21–24.

[31] CAL. HEALTH & SAFETY CODE § 1279.1 (Deering 2007); FLA. STAT. ANN. § 195.1051 (LEXISNEXIS 2007); NEV. REV. STAT. ANN. SEC 439.855 (LEXISNEXIS 2007); N.J. STAT. AN. SEC 26:2H-12.25 (LEXISNEXIS 2007); 2003 OR. LAWS ch. 686, sec 4); 40 P.S. sec 1303.308 (2006); VT. STAT. ANN. tit. 18, sec 1915 (2007); WASH. REV. CODE ANN. SEC 70.41.380 (LEXISNEXIS 2007).

[32] 40 P.S. § 1303.308 (2006).

[33] Kraman, S., MD, and Hamm, G., JD. "Risk Management: Extreme Honesty May Be the Best Policy." *Annals of Internal Medicine* 1999, 131: 963–967.

[34] Department of Veterans Affairs, Veterans Health Administration. VHA Directive 2005-049, Disclosure of Adverse Events to Patients, October 27, 2005.

[35] Richard C. Boothman. "The University of Michigan Health System's Claims Experience…and the importance of open disclosure." Presentation to the New Jersey Council of Teaching Hospitals, October 4, 2006.

[36] Richard C. Boothman, Chief Risk Officer, University of Michigan Health System. Testimony before the U.S. Senate Committee on Health, Education, Labor and Pensions Committee, June 22, 2006.

[37] Ibid.

[38] Ibid.

[39] Ibid.

[40] American Tort Reform Association. "Judicial Hellholes" Report. 2006. (accessible at http://www.atra.org/reports/hellholes/report.pdf) (last visited October 10, 2007).

[41] McDonald T. Presentation: "Full Disclosure: One Hospital's Experience." University of Illinois Medical Center. March 9, 2007, at the Chicago Patient Safety Forum's Annual Meeting in Chicago, IL.

[42] Miller K. "A Sorry State." *Las Vegas Life*, July 2007.

[43] Kowalczyk L. "Hospitals Study When to Apologize to Patients." *Boston Globe*, July 24, 2005.

[44] "COPIC's 3Rs Program, Recognize, Respond to, and Resolve Patient Injuries." Richard Quinn, 3Rs Medical Director, COPIC Insurance Company.

[45] Ibid.

[46] Driver J. Presentation to the Greater New York Hosp. Ass'n., May 2005.

[47] See O'Reilly KB. "Harvard Adopts a Disclosure and Apology Policy." AMNews. June 12, 2006.

[48] Wojcieszak D, Banja J, Houk C. "The Sorry Works! Coalition: Making the Case for Full-Disclosure." *The Joint Commission Journal on Quality and Patient Safety*. (June 2006).

[49] Eisenberg D. "When Doctors Say, 'We're Sorry.'" *Time Magazine*, August 15, 2005.

[50] It is this type of program that the authors have created for healthcare organizations nationwide.

[51] JCAHO. "Ethics, Rights, and Responsibilities," in *Comprehensive Accreditation Manual for Hospitals: The Official Handbook* (Oakbrook Terrace, Ill.: JCAHO 2003), Patient Rights Standard RI. 2.90, RI-12.